Origami Symphony No. 10

Lucky & Dangerous Sides of Origami

Books by John Montroll
www.johnmontroll.com
Instagram: @montrollorigami

Origami Symphonies

Origami Symphony No. 1: The Elephant's Trumpet Call
Origami Symphony No. 2: Trio of Sharks & Playful Prehistoric Mammals
Origami Symphony No. 3: Duet of Majestic Dragons & Dinosaurs
Origami Symphony No. 4: Capturing Vibrant Coral Reef Fish
Origami Symphony No. 5: Woodwinds, Horns, and a Moose
Origami Symphony No. 6: Striped Snakes Changing Scales
Origami Symphony No. 7: Musical Monkeys
Origami Symphony No. 8: An Octet of Cats
Origami Symphony No. 9: Ode to Australia
Origami Symphony No. 10: Lucky & Dangerous Sides of Origami

General Origami

Origami Fold-by-Fold
DC Super Heroes Origami
Origami Worldwide
Teach Yourself Origami: Third Edition
Christmas Origami: Second Edition
Storytime Origami
Origami Inside-Out: Third Edition

Animal Origami

Arctic Animals in Origami
Origami Aquarium
Dogs in Origami
Perfect Pets Origami
Dragons and Other Fantastic Creatures in Origami
Bugs in Origami
Horses in Origami: Second Edition
Origami Birds: Second Edition
Origami Gone Wild
Dinosaur Origami
Origami Dinosaurs for Beginners
Prehistoric Origami: Dinosaurs and other Creatures: Third Edition
Mythological Creatures and the Chinese Zodiac Origami
Origami Sea Life: Third Edition
Bringing Origami to Life: Second Edition
Origami Sculptures: Fourth Edition
African Animals in Origami: Third Edition
North American Animals in Origami: Third Edition
Origami for the Enthusiast: Second Edition
Animal Origami for the Enthusiast: Second Edition

Geometric Origami

Origami Stars: Second Edition
Galaxy of Origami Stars: Second Edition
Origami and Math: Simple to Complex: Second Edition
Origami & Geometry
3D Origami Platonic Solids & More: Second Edition
3D Origami Diamonds
3D Origami Antidiamonds
3D Origami Pyramids
A Plethora of Polyhedra in Origami: Third Edition
Classic Polyhedra Origami
A Constellation of Origami Polyhedra
Origami Polyhedra Design

Dollar Bill Origami

Dollar Origami Treasures: Second Edition
Dollar Bill Animals in Origami: Second Revised Edition
Dollar Bill Origami
Easy Dollar Bill Origami

Simple Origami

Fun and Simple Origami: 101 Easy-to-Fold Projects: Second Edition
Origami Twelve Days of Christmas: And Santa, Too!
Super Simple Origami
Easy Dollar Bill Origami
Easy Origami
Easy Origami 2
Easy Origami 3
Easy Origami Coloring Book
Easy Origami Animals
Easy Origami Polar Animals
Easy Origami Ocean Animals
Easy Origami Woodland Animals
Easy Origami Jungle Animals
Meditative Origami

Origami Symphony No. 10

Lucky & Dangerous Sides of Origami

Antroll Publishing Company

John Montroll

To Andy, Barbara Anne, Sarah, and Elliott

Origami Symphony No. 10: *Lucky & Dangerous Sides of Origami*

ISBN-10: 1-877656-65-8
ISBN-13: 978-1-877656-65-1

Antroll Publishing Company

Introduction

Welcome to the world premier of the Tenth Origami Symphony! Based on a four movement musical symphony, many themes and styles demonstrate the power of origami. Horses, elephants, butterflies, three-dimensional diamonds, and large animals are presented in stunning detail.

Within the four movements are 36 models. The first movement contains several horse and elephant designs. Horse variations include a Unicorn, Pegasus, and Donkey. Elephants from simple to complex are shown, including the detailed African Elephant. The second movement highlights peaceful animals that bring good luck. This includes a couple of butterflies, swans, a Cardinal and an intricate Panda. A collection of three-dimensional diamonds and colorful octahedra shows the geometric side of origami. The symphony concludes with more complex animals. A Lion, Lioness, Rhino, and Hyena show an expressive side of origami.

The models were designed to be easily foldable from standard origami paper. Despite their complexity, all the models are diagrammed in under 40 steps. I have pioneered the style of using efficiency with design so the models can be folded in far fewer steps than expected. The symphony opens with a detailed horse which is accomplished in only 21 steps. The efficiency and ease in folding detailed animals adds a new dimension to the art of origami.

The diagrams are drawn in the internationally approved Randlett-Yoshizawa style. You can use any kind of square paper for these models, but the best results will be achieved with standard origami paper, which is colored on one side and white on the other (in the diagrams in this book, the shading represents the colored side). Large sheets, such as nine inches squared, are easier to use than small ones.

Origami supplies can be found in arts and craft shops, or at Dover Publications online: www.doverpublications.com. You can also visit OrigamiUSA at www.origamiusa.org for origami supplies and other related information including an extensive list of local, national, and international origami groups.

Please follow me on Instagram @montrollorigami to see posts of my origami.

I thank my editor, Charley Montroll. I also thank the folders who proof-read the diagrams and continued to encourage me to present origami in symphonic form.

I hope you enjoy the many challenges and styles from Origami Symphony No. 10.

John Montroll
www.johnmontroll.com

Contents

★ Simple
★★ Intermediate
★★★ Complex
★★★★ Very Complex

First Movement
Allegro: Theme & Variation on the Horse & Elephant

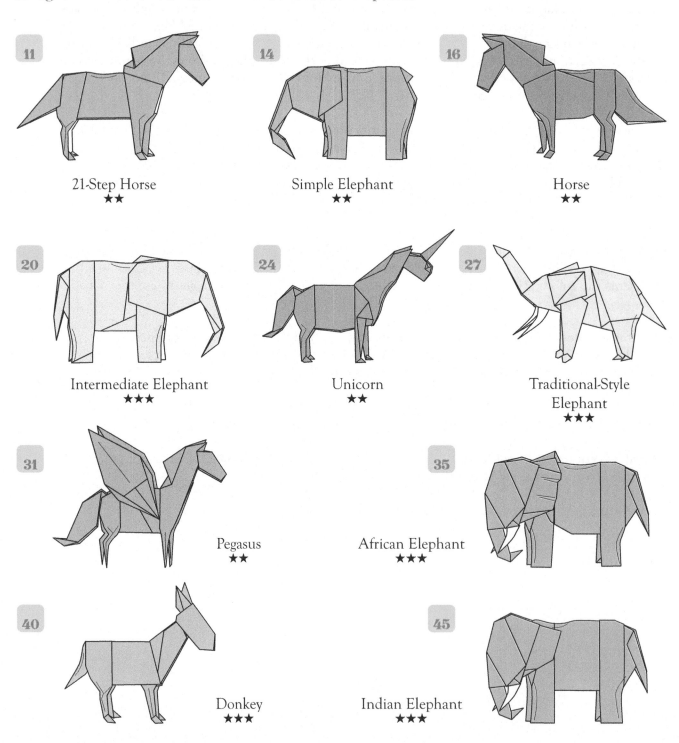

11 — 21-Step Horse
★★

14 — Simple Elephant
★★

16 — Horse
★★

20 — Intermediate Elephant
★★★

24 — Unicorn
★★

27 — Traditional-Style Elephant
★★★

31 — Pegasus
★★

35 — African Elephant
★★★

40 — Donkey
★★★

45 — Indian Elephant
★★★

Second Movement
Andante: Animals That Bring Good Luck

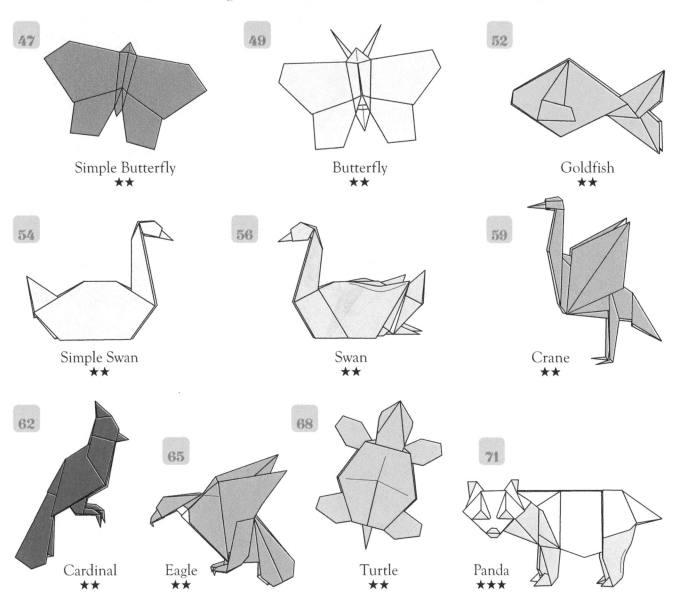

47 Simple Butterfly ★★

49 Butterfly ★★

52 Goldfish ★★

54 Simple Swan ★★

56 Swan ★★

59 Crane ★★

62 Cardinal ★★

65 Eagle ★★

68 Turtle ★★

71 Panda ★★★

Third Movement
Minuet of Lucky Diamonds with a Trio of Colorful Octahedra

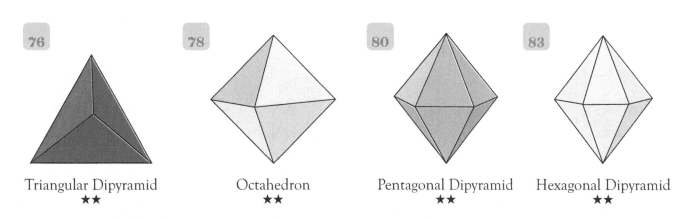

76 Triangular Dipyramid ★★

78 Octahedron ★★

80 Pentagonal Dipyramid ★★

83 Hexagonal Dipyramid ★★

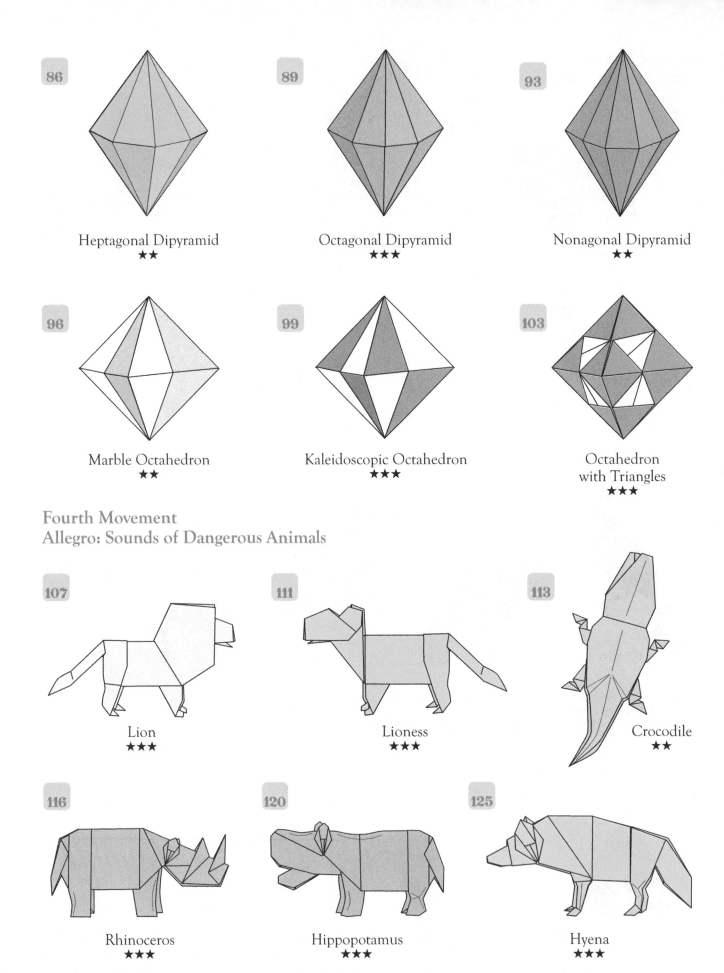

86 Heptagonal Dipyramid
★★

89 Octagonal Dipyramid
★★★

93 Nonagonal Dipyramid
★★

96 Marble Octahedron
★★

99 Kaleidoscopic Octahedron
★★★

103 Octahedron
with Triangles
★★★

Fourth Movement
Allegro: Sounds of Dangerous Animals

107 Lion
★★★

111 Lioness
★★★

113 Crocodile
★★

116 Rhinoceros
★★★

120 Hippopotamus
★★★

125 Hyena
★★★

Symbols

Lines	Arrows	
— — — — — — — — Valley fold, fold in front.	⌢→ Fold in this direction.	↩→ Turn over.
—·—·—·—·—·—·— Mountain fold, fold behind.	⌢▷ Fold behind.	⇨ Sink or three dimensional folding.
———————— Crease line.	⌢▷ Unfold.	
············· X-ray or guide line.	◁⌢▷ Fold and unfold.	⇨ Place your finger between these layers.

Origami Elephants

I have always been fascinated with elephants as being majestic and unique animals. A trunk for a four-legged animal gives it super-powers; an elephant can kill a lion with its trunk or pick up and return a shoe to a child. I've had a few rides on elephants in India, and they are surprisingly tall. Elephants symbolize good luck and prosperity, strength and power, loyalty and wisdom, nobility and dignity, a gentle nature and triumphs. Their distinct shape plus simple geometric outlines makes them ideal for art and especially for origami design.

As one of the most popular origami subjects, I have seen many designs for elephants throughout the history of origami. I've seen older versions from two sheets, several requiring cuts and some with three legs, yet they all share the distinct elephant shape. More recently, designers have shown many versions from one square. Some are simple and abstract, some depict the head, many highlight artistically thick legs and some are designed with or without tusks. These designs range from simple to complex to super-complex and all levels of realism.

I have more elephant designs than any other subject. The first three origami books I wrote contained elephants. Each had the detail of white tusks. It is the simple detail of white tusks that has added so much to the magic of design. As I continued writing origami books, if an elephant would fit the theme, it would be there.

Designing elephants is quite challenging. It requires much detail and many parts including large ears, the four legs, the trunk and possible tusks which are fun to show as white. With all this detail, there has to be some consideration to the thickness and complexity of the model. My designs show an evolution to my work. Each represents my understanding and take on origami design at that time, in my continuing quest to discover more about the possibilities of origami.

I am always searching for better ways to capture a subject, including easier ways to fold an animal with the same or similar detail to my previous work. Rather than think about where all the legs and other appendages would be on the square sheet, I am looking for structures that allow many parts to naturally fit together. Sometimes I use math to capture the proportion of the animal in an efficient way.

For this book, I am glad to show a variety of elephants with varying detail. I am most proud of the African Elephant, not only for the intricate shape, but indeed its spirit when folded from kami, all accomplished in under 40 rather unusual steps. I hope you enjoy this work, too.

Origami Symphony No. 10

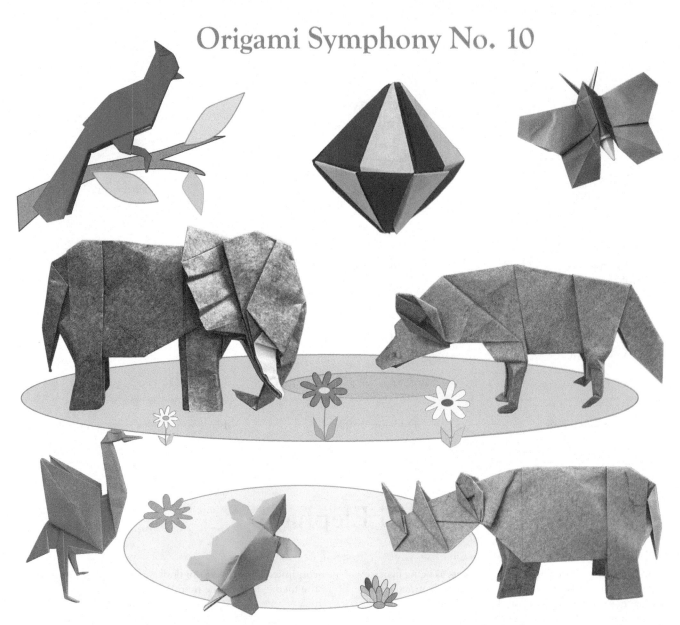

This is a lucky symphony. This is a dangerous symphony. Butterflies, swans, a turtle and panda bring good luck. Several three-dimensional diamonds grant many wishes. Yet hidden in the trees and water lurk lions, crocodiles and hyenas.

This is also a majestic symphony. The first movement is dedicated to horses and elephants through theme and variation. The first model, the 21-Step Horse, makes a bold statement; using clever design techniques, the detailed horse is folded in far fewer steps than expected, and foreshadows the rest of the symphony. A Unicorn, Pegasus, and Donkey each have a song to sing. A parade of elephants, from simple to complex march through, ending with the majestic pair of African and Indian Elephants.

For the second movement, Allegro: Animals that Bring Good Luck include butterflies and swans, a Goldfish, Crane, and Panda. Along with a Cardinal, Eagle, and Turtle, these models show the peaceful side of origami. Using colorful papers that represent the animals add an element of realism.

More luck is found in the third movement, Minuet of Lucky Diamonds with a Trio of Colorful Octahedra. This series of diamonds have a polygonal base at the equator, ranging from triangular to nonagonal. In particular, the ones from a pentagonal to nonagonal bases use similar folding methods, bringing unity to this style of folding. The trio shows mind-boggling models with fancy color-change patterns embedded on the octahedron.

The fourth movement ends the symphony with Sounds of Dangerous Animals. A majestic Lion and Lioness are basking in the heat. A Crocodile and Hippo are splashing in the water while a Rhino and Hyena are exploring the landscape. Fold these carefully and quietly, as these dangerous animals do not want to be disturbed.

Majestic, lucky and dangerous animals along with three-dimensional diamonds fill this symphony with variety. Capturing each of these models in under 40 steps adds to the folding experience. I hope you enjoy these challenging origami designs.

First Movement

Allegro: Theme & Variation on the Horse & Elephant

Plenty of horse neighs and elephant trumpet calls fill this majestic movement. Starting with the 21-Step Horse and a Simple Elephant, each variation becomes more challenging. A Unicorn and Pegasus trots and flies away. A Donkey sings a humorous tune. Increasing complexity leads to magnificent African and Indian Elephants.

21-Step Horse

Horses can read human emotions and have been with us for thousand of years. They have inspired art depictions through the ages. From cave drawings to famous paintings, horse portraits to sculptures, horses have been represented in art more than any other animal. Origami is also a perfect medium and there are many origami horse designs, found around the world. This 21-step Horse explores efficiency in design as a fun way to capture this subject.

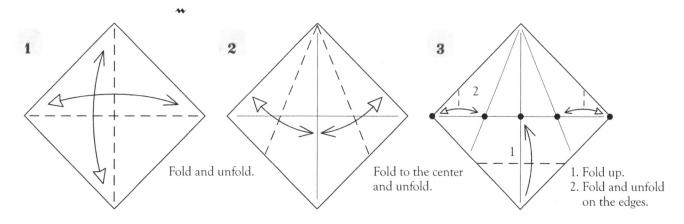

1

2 Fold and unfold.

3 Fold to the center and unfold.

1. Fold up.
2. Fold and unfold on the edges.

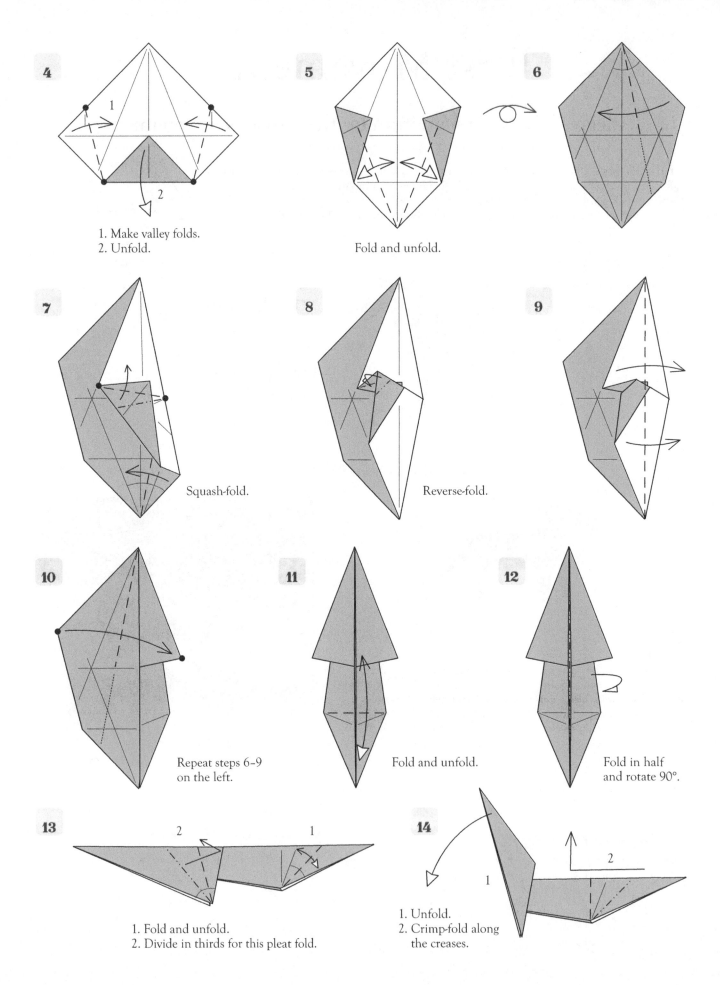

4

1. Make valley folds.
2. Unfold.

5

Fold and unfold.

6

7

Squash-fold.

8

Reverse-fold.

9

10

Repeat steps 6–9
on the left.

11

Fold and unfold.

12

Fold in half
and rotate 90°.

13

2   1

1. Fold and unfold.
2. Divide in thirds for this pleat fold.

14

1

2

1. Unfold.
2. Crimp-fold along
   the creases.

15

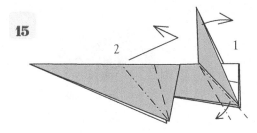

1. Crimp-fold.
2. Crimp-fold along the creases.

16

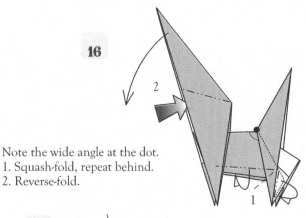

Note the wide angle at the dot.
1. Squash-fold, repeat behind.
2. Reverse-fold.

17

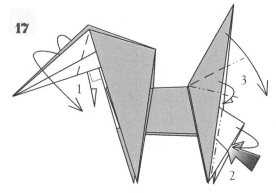

1. Note the right angle. Outside-reverse-fold.
2. Reverse-fold.
3. Crimp-fold.

18

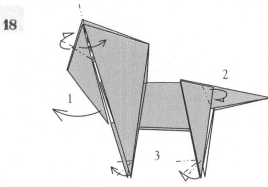

1. Crimp-fold.
2. Mountain-fold, repeat behind.
3. Make squash folds, repeat behind.

19

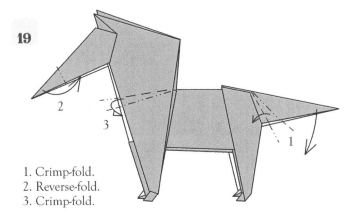

1. Crimp-fold.
2. Reverse-fold.
3. Crimp-fold.

20

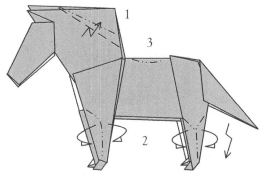

1. Pleat-fold.
2. Thin and shape the legs, repeat behind.
3. Shape the back.

21

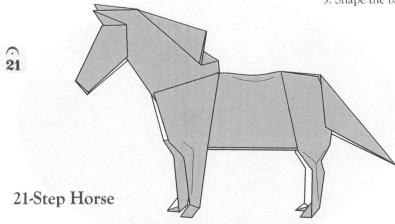

21-Step Horse

Simple Elephant

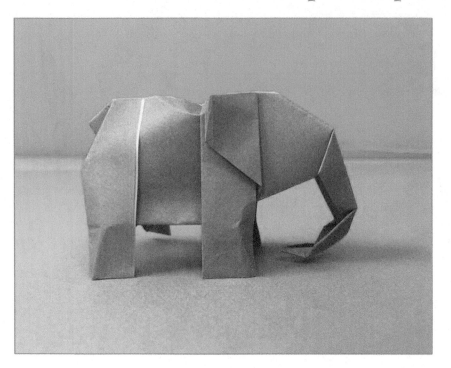

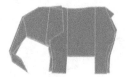

As the world's largest land animal, elephants can live for up to 60-70 years. Elephants spend 3/4 of the day eating grasses, leaves, fruits, roots and even woody parts of trees. These intelligent mammals have a variety of personalities including playfulness, gentleness, and leadership.

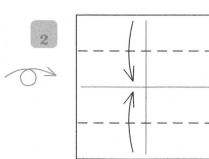

1
Fold and unfold.

2
Fold to the center.

3
1. Fold and unfold.
2. Fold the top layer and unfold.

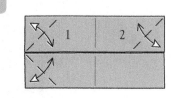

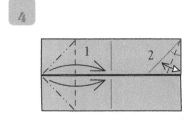

4
1. Make squash folds.
2. Fold the top layer and unfold.

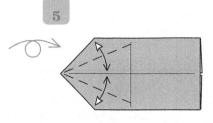

5
Fold to the center and unfold.

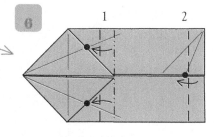

6
1. Pleat-fold so the mountain line meets the dots.
2. Fold slightly to the right of the dot.

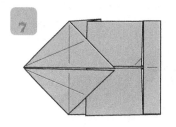

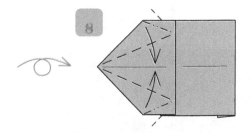

Make squash folds.

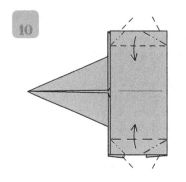

Pleat-fold.

Make petal folds.

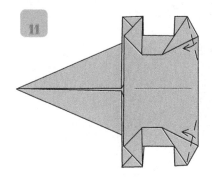

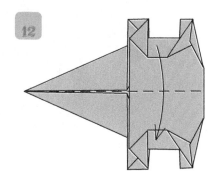

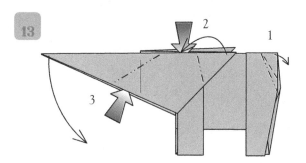

1. Crimp-fold.
2. Reverse-fold, repeat behind.
3. Reverse-fold.

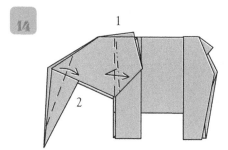

1. Pleat-fold.
2. Valley-fold.
Repeat behind.

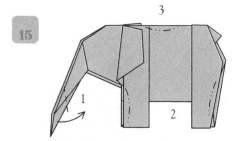

1. Outside-reverse-fold.
2. Shape the legs, repeat behind.
3. Shape the back.

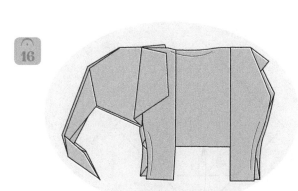

Simple Elephant

Horse

Horses are majestic herd animals that like plenty of company. Records show they were domesticated over 3,000 years ago but probably 10,000 years ago. Our civilization depended on the horse. Always on the lookout for predators they can see almost 360 degrees around them and can hear far better than humans. As one of the fastest land animals, horses can gallop at speeds of 40 miles per hour.

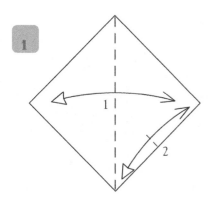

1. Fold and unfold.
2. Fold and unfold on the edge.

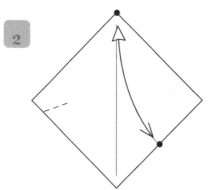

Fold and unfold on the edge.

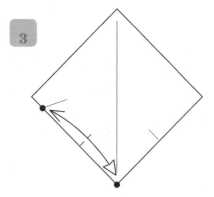

Fold and unfold on the edge.

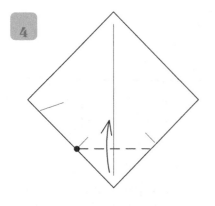

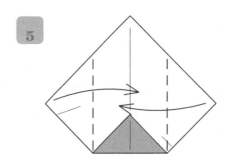

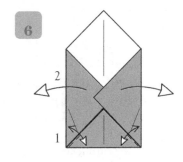

1. Fold and unfold.
2. Unfold.

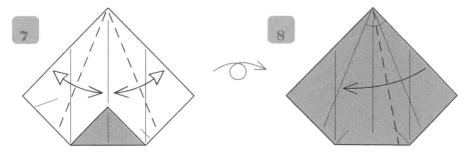

7 Fold and unfold.

8 Bring the edge to the crease.

9

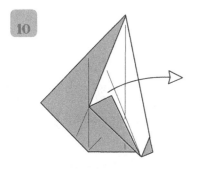

10 Unfold.

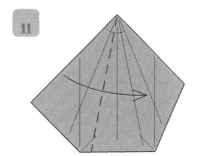

11 Repeat steps 8–10 on the left.

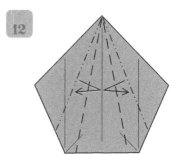

12 Pleat-fold along the creases.

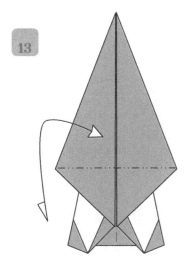

13 Fold and unfold.

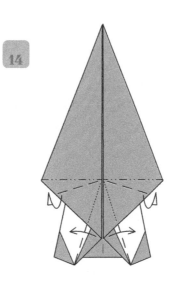

14

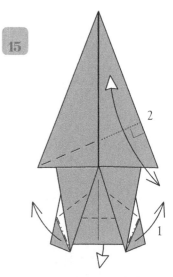

15
1. Petal-fold and swing out from behind.
2. Fold and unfold.

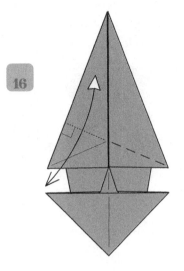

16

Fold and unfold.
Rotate 90°.

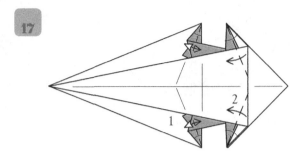

17

1. Fold and unfold.
2. Make valley folds.

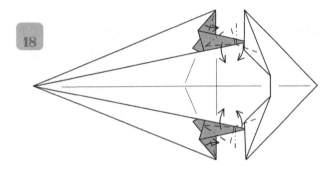

18

Make squash folds.

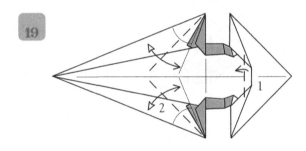

19

1. Fold the top flap.
2. Fold and unfold.

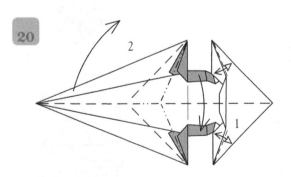

20

1. Fold and unfold.
2. Fold in half and
   crimp-fold on the left.

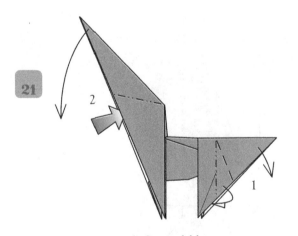

21

1. Crimp-fold.
2. Reverse-fold.

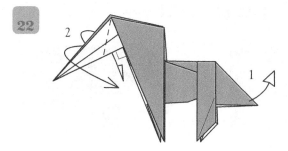

22

1. Unfold.
2. Note the right angle.
   Outside-reverse-fold.

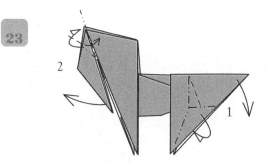

23

1. Fold along some of the
   creases to form the tail.
2. Crimp-fold.

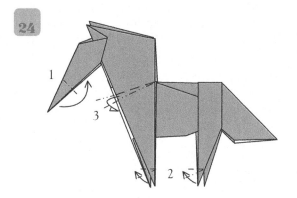

24

1. Reverse-fold.
2. Make squash folds,
   repeat behind.
3. Crimp-fold.

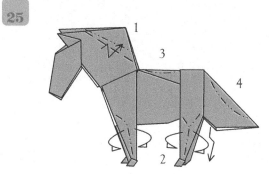

25

1. Pleat-fold.
2. Thin and shape the legs,
   repeat behind.
3. Shape the back.
4. Shape the tail.

26

Horse

Intermediate Elephant

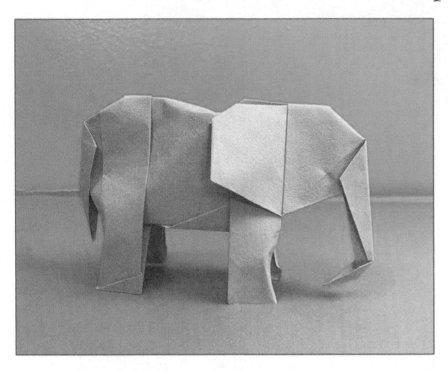

Of all the four-legged animals, elephants have a super-power: their trunk. A trunk has 150,000 muscles which is used as a hand, tool for gathering food, a snorkel when swimming, and can pull apart parts of trees and vegetation. They use their trunks as a glass to pick up water, then pour into their mouths. An elephant can use its trunk to kill a lion or pick up a coin.

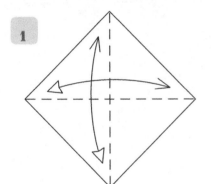

Fold and unfold.

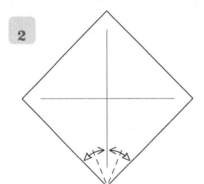

Fold and unfold on the bottom.

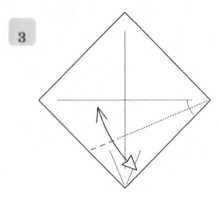

Fold and unfold on the edge.

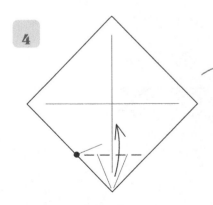

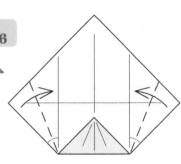

Fold and unfold to make two vertical lines.

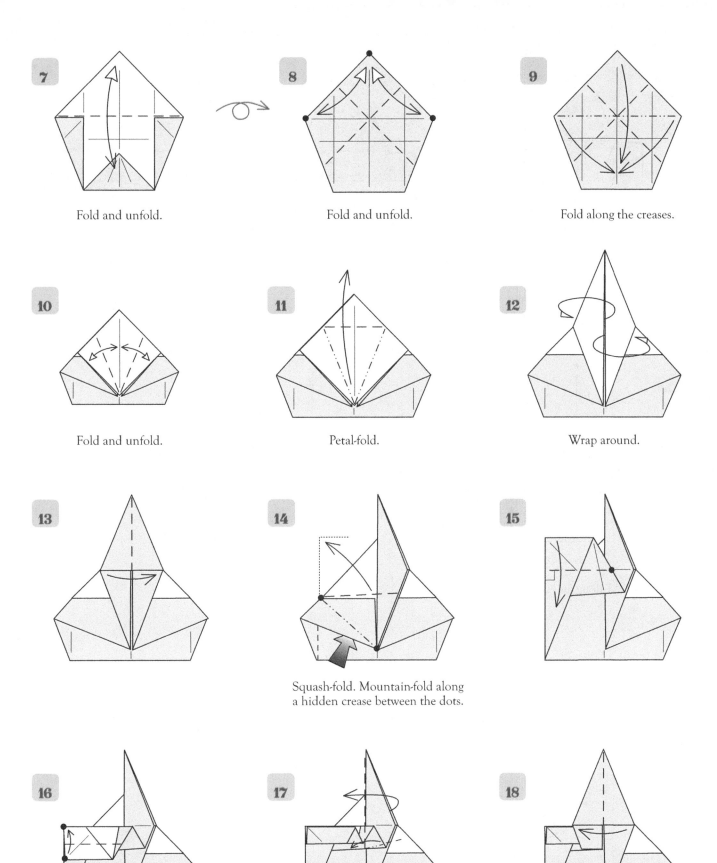

7 Fold and unfold.

8 Fold and unfold.

9 Fold along the creases.

10 Fold and unfold.

11 Petal-fold.

12 Wrap around.

13

14 Squash-fold. Mountain-fold along a hidden crease between the dots.

15

16

17 Make a small squash fold.

18 Repeat steps 13–17 on the right.

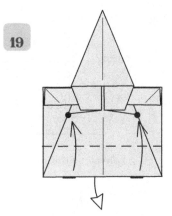

19

Bring the edge to the dots
and swing out from behind.

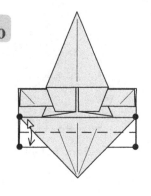

20

Fold and unfold
the top flap.

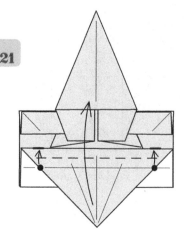

21

Fold the top layer up.

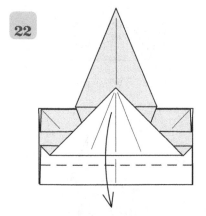

22

Fold along the crease.

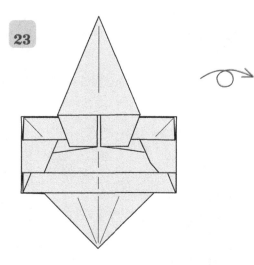

23

Rotate 90°.

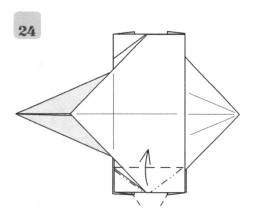

24

Petal-fold.

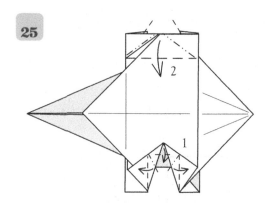

25

1. Petal-fold.
2. Repeat steps 24–25
   on the top.

26

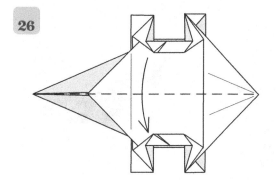

27

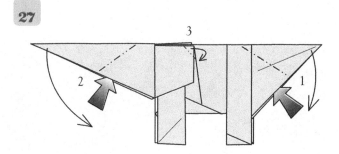

1. Reverse-fold.
2. Reverse-fold.
3. Reverse-fold, repeat behind.

28

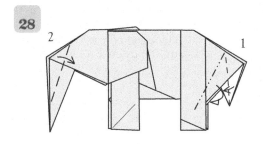

1. Reverse-fold.
2. Valley-fold.
Repeat behind.

29

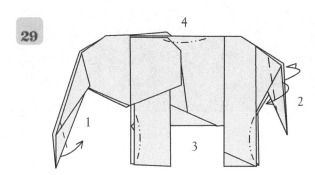

1. Outside-reverse-fold.
2. Outside-reverse-fold.
3. Shape the legs, repeat behind.
4. Shape the back.

30

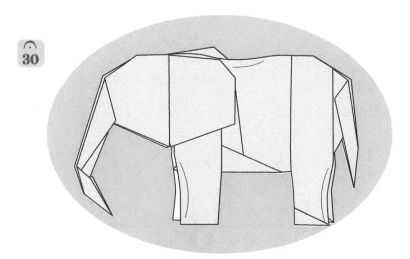

Intermediate Elephant

Unicorn

Many cultures created their versions of unicorns. The horn is called an alicorn and a baby unicorn is a sparkle. In Chinese mythology, the unicorn is a Qilin. Unicorns dwell deep in woods or forests. They have magical powers that can heal wounds and allow them to fly. They are a symbol of innocence, masculinity and power. In today's world unicorns inspire endless possibilities.

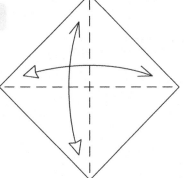

Fold and unfold.

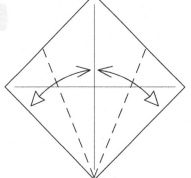

Fold to the center and unfold.

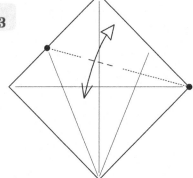

Fold and unfold on the diagonal.

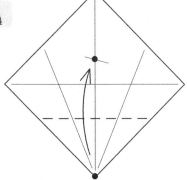

The dots will meet.

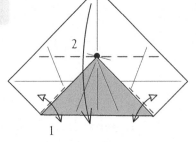

1. Fold and unfold on the left and right.
2. Fold down.

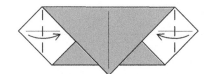

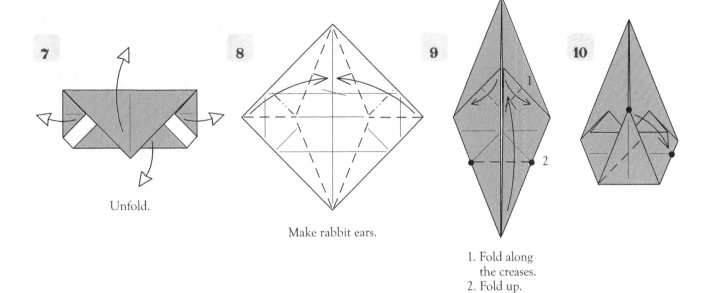

7

Unfold.

8

Make rabbit ears.

9

1. Fold along
   the creases.
2. Fold up.

10

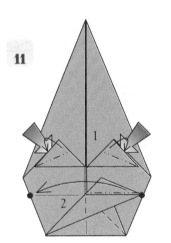

11

1. Make reverse folds.
2. Squash-fold.

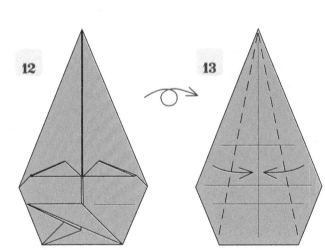

12

13

Fold to the center.

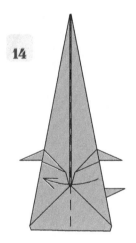

14

Fold in half and
rotate 90°.

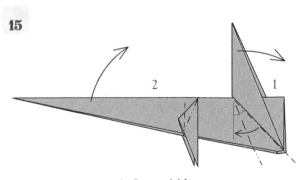

15

1. Crimp-fold.
2. Crimp-fold.

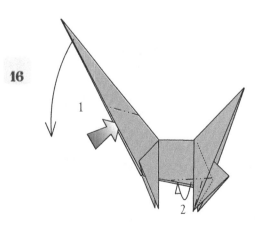

16

1. Reverse-fold.
2. Fold the hidden layers,
   repeat behind.

17

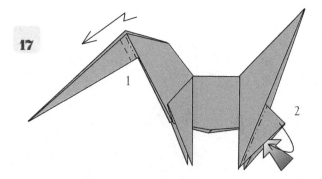

1. Crimp-fold.
2. Reverse-fold.

18

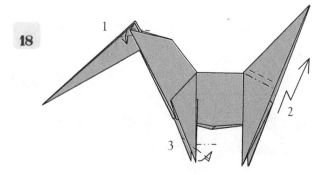

1. Reverse-fold, repeat behind.
2. Crimp-fold.
3. Squash-fold, repeat behind.

19

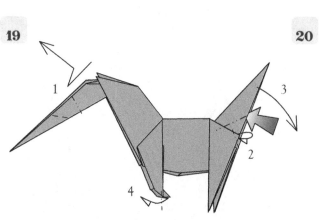

1. Crimp-fold.
2. Fold inside, repeat behind.
3. Reverse-fold.
4. Mountain-fold, repeat behind.

20

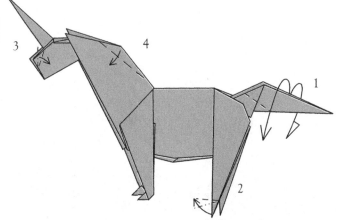

1. Outside-reverse-fold.
2. Squash-fold, repeat behind.
3. Squash-fold, repeat behind.
4. Valley-fold.

21

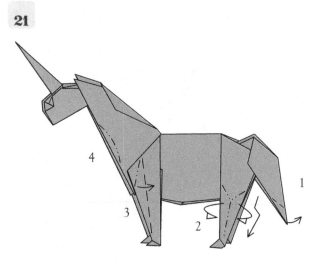

1. Outside-reverse-fold.
2. Shape the legs, repeat behind.
3. Squash-fold, repeat behind.
4. Shape the neck, repeat behind.

22

Unicorn

Traditional-Style Elephant

The elephant has the best sense of smell than any other animal. With 2,000 genes specialized to detect odors, that is twice as much as for a dog. The rat used to hold the record for the best sense of smell. Elephants often carry their trunks pointing upward to be able to sense more smells. They can detect water 12 miles away.

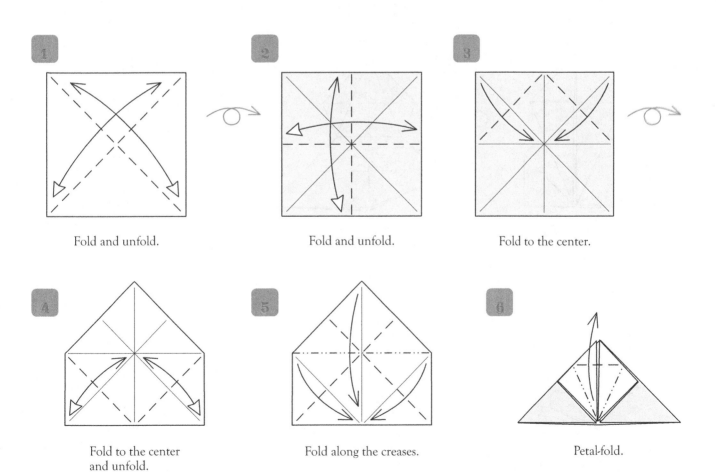

1. Fold and unfold.

2. Fold and unfold.

3. Fold to the center.

4. Fold to the center and unfold.

5. Fold along the creases.

6. Petal-fold.

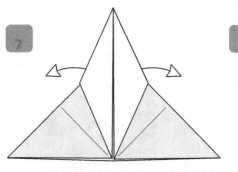

Pull out the hidden corners.

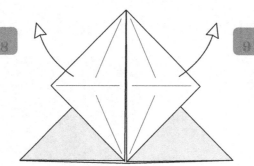

Unfold everything.

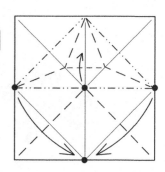

Fold along the creases. Puff out at the dot in the center. The other three dots will meet at the bottom.

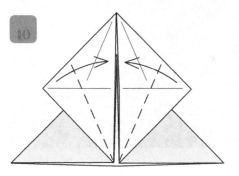

Fold to the center.

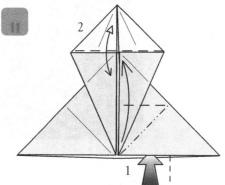
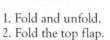

1. Squash-fold.
2. Fold and unfold.

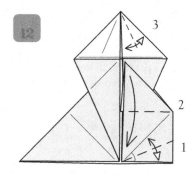

1. Fold and unfold.
2. Fold down.
3. Fold and unfold.

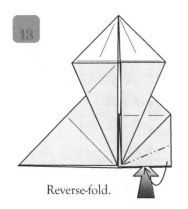

Reverse-fold.

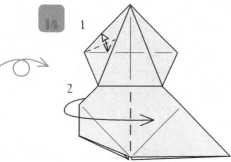

1. Fold and unfold.
2. Fold the top flap.

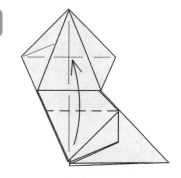

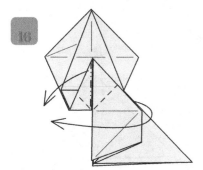

This is similar to a reverse fold.

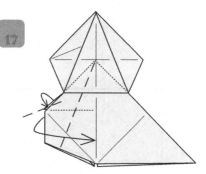

Squash-fold.

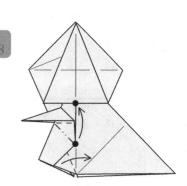

Squash-fold.

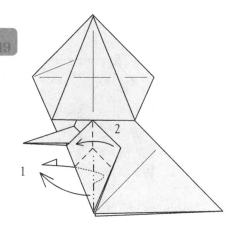

This combination begins with an outside-reverse fold at 1, then continue at 2.

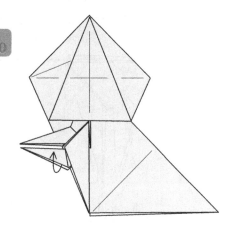

Wrap around to make the flap white.

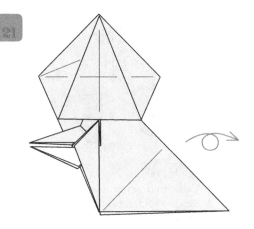

Repeat steps 11–20 in the opposite direction.

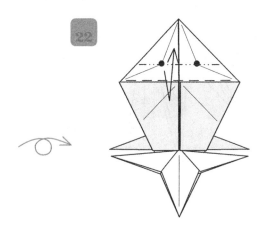

Pleat-fold.

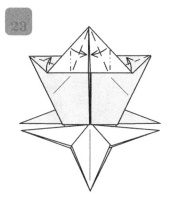

Make squash folds.

Bring the darker paper to the front.

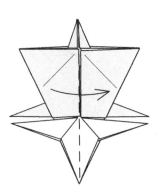

Fold in half and rotate.

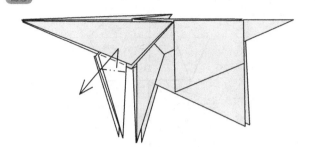

26

Pleat-fold, repeat behind.

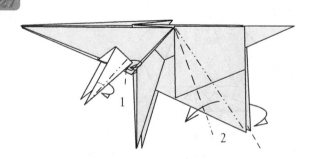

27

1. Thin the tusk at an angle of 1/3, repeat behind.
2. Crimp-fold.

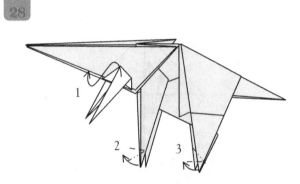

28

1. Tuck inside.
2. Spead the paper.
3. Crimp-fold.
Repeat behind.

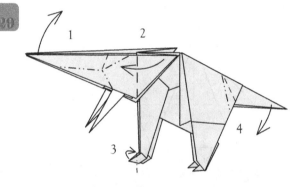

29

1. Double-rabbit-ear.
2. Valley-fold, repeat behind.
3. Reverse-fold, repeat behind.
4. Crimp-fold.

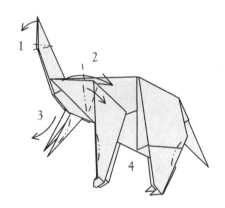

30

1. Crimp-fold.
2. Squash-fold.
3. Curl the tusks.
4. Shape the legs.
Repeat behind at 2, 3, and 4.

31

Traditional-Style Elephant

Pegasus

Pegasus is the flying horse from Greek mythology. It is a symbol of inspiration, artistic creativity, and the poetic arts. It has certainly given origami designers a lot of fun, as there are many origami renditions of Pegasus, from simple to super-duper complex.

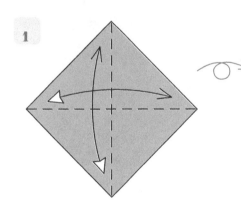

Fold and unfold.

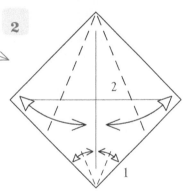

1. Fold and unfold on the bottom.
2. Fold and unfold.

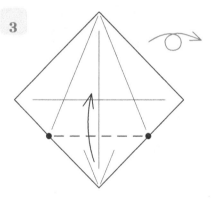

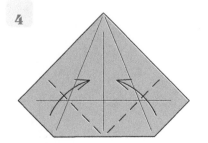

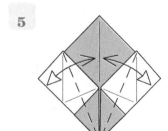

Fold to the center and unfold.

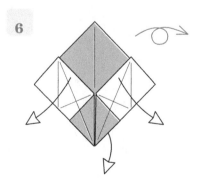

Unfold everything.

7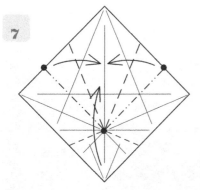

Fold along the creases.
Puff in at the lower dot,
the upper dots will meet.

8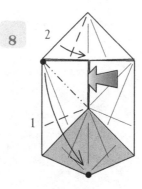

This is a combination
of two squash folds.

9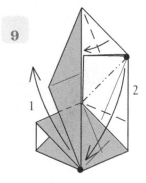

1. Fold up.
2. Repeat steps 8–9
   on the right.

10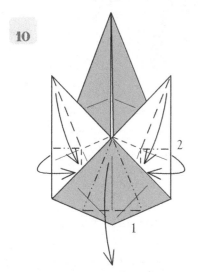

1. Petal-fold.
2. Continue with
   squash folds.

11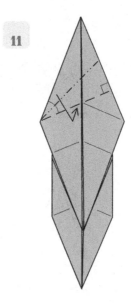

Pleat-fold. Valley-fold
along the crease.

12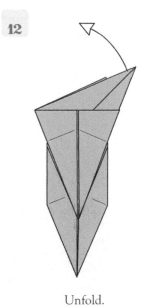

Unfold.

13

Repeat steps 11–12
on the right.

14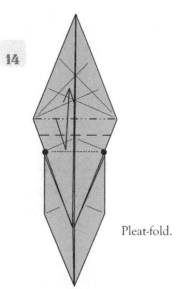

Pleat-fold.

15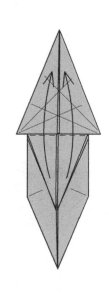

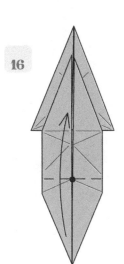

16

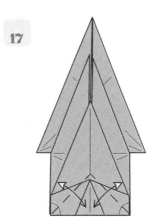

17

Fold and unfold
the top flap.

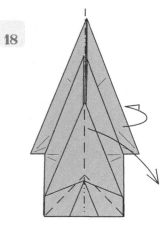

18

Fold the tail while folding
in half. Rotate 90°.

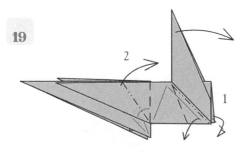

19

1. Crimp-fold.
2. Repeat behind.

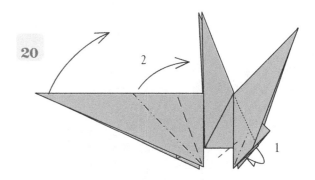

20

1. Reverse-fold the hidden layer,
   repeat behind.
2. Crimp-fold along the creases.

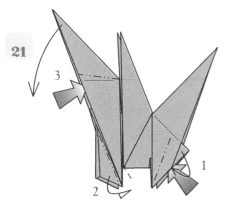

21

1. Reverse-fold.
2. Reverse-fold, repeat behind.
3. Reverse-fold.

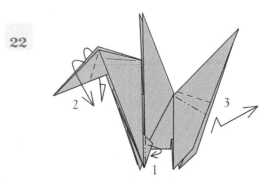

22

1. Reverse-fold, repeat behind.
2. Outside-reverse-fold.
3. Crimp-fold.

23

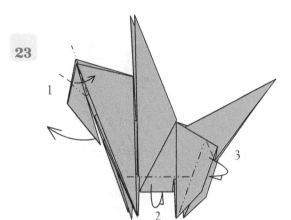

1. Crimp-fold.
2. Fold inside, repeat behind.
3. Reverse-fold, repeat behind.

24

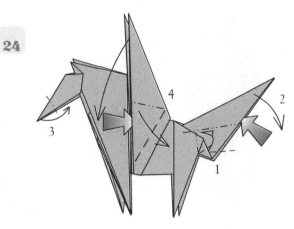

1. Fold inside, repeat behind.
2. Reverse-fold.
3. Reverse-fold.
4. Squash-fold, repeat behind.

25

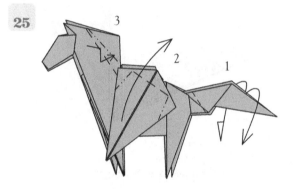

1. Outside-reverse-fold.
2. Petal-fold, repeat behind.
3. Pleat-fold all the layers.

26

1. Outside-revese-fold.
2. Thin and shape the legs, repeat behind.

27

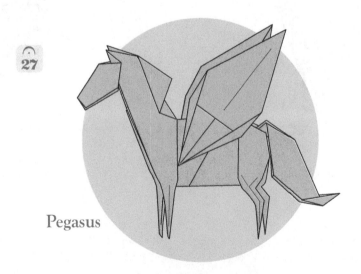

Pegasus

African Elephant

The African elephant is the largest land animal with a height of 10 feet tall. Compared to the Indian elephant, the ears are larger and they have two finger-like tips on their trunk, as opposed to one finger for the Indian elephant. These elephants clear pathways in dense forests that allow passage for other species while their footprints are often filled with water that creates new ecosystems for tadpoles and other small creatures.

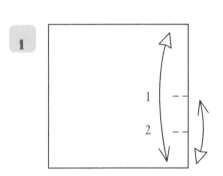

Fold and unfold on the edge.

Fold and unfold on the top.

1. Fold and unfold on the left.
2. Fold and unfold. Rotate the left dot to the bottom.

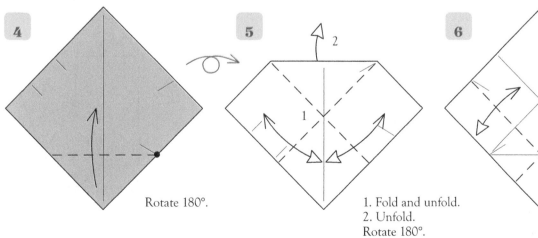

Rotate 180°.

1. Fold and unfold.
2. Unfold.
Rotate 180°.

Fold and unfold.

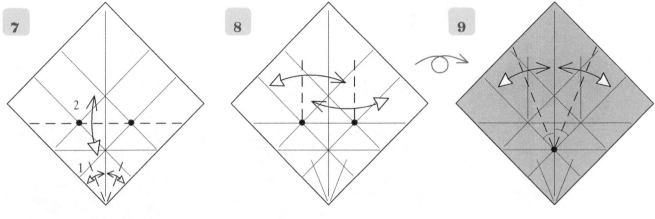

7

Fold and unfold at 1 and 2.

8

Fold and unfold.

9

Fold and unfold.

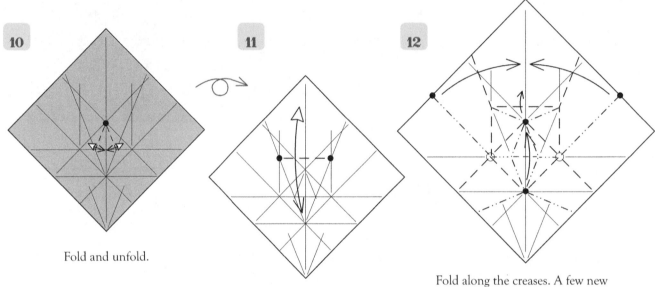

10

Fold and unfold.

11

Fold and unfold.

12

Fold along the creases. A few new ones will be made by folding.
1. Push in at the small circles, these will meet near the bottom.
2. Puff out at the two dots in the center, these will meet.
3. The upper dots will meet.

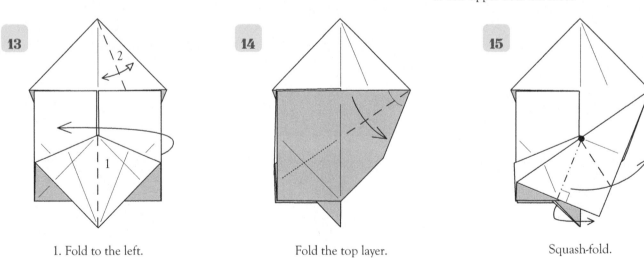

13

1. Fold to the left.
2. Fold and unfold.

14

Fold the top layer.

15

Squash-fold.

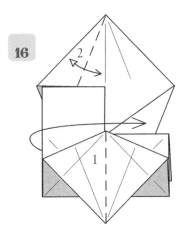

16

Repeat steps 13–15
on the left.

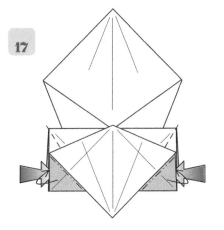

17

Make reverse folds.

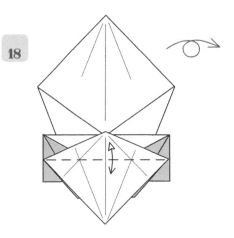

18

Fold and unfold the
top flap. Rotate 180°.

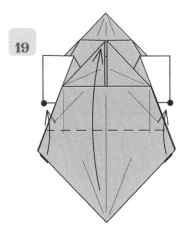

19

Bring the edges
to the dots.

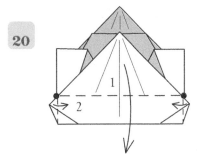

20

1. Fold down.
2. Fold on the sides.

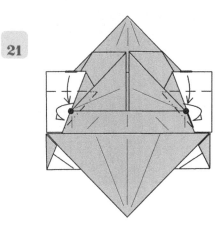

21

Reverse-fold down
to the dots.

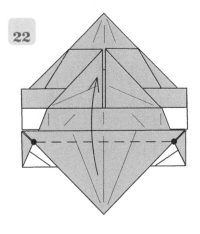

22

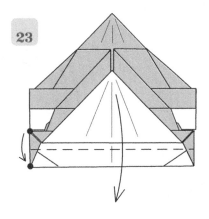

23

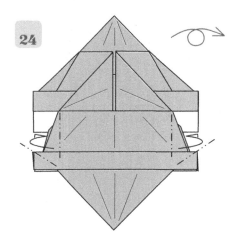

24

Make squash folds.

African Elephant **37**

25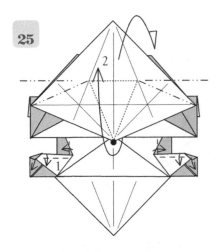

1. Make small squash folds and spread slightly at the corners.
2. Fold behind and make squash folds on hidden layers. Lift up at the dot so it goes to the top.

26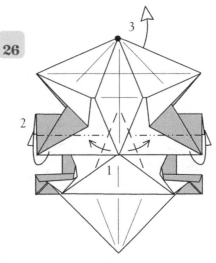

1. Fold the flap and then
2. Tuck inside. Repeat 1 and 2 on the right.
3. Lift up from behind and push in at the dot.

27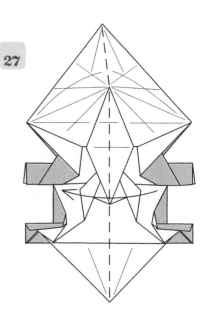

Fold in half and rotate 90°.

28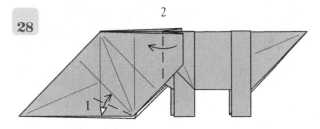

1. Fold and unfold.
2. Fold the ear.
Repeat behind.

29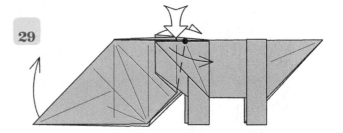

Push in at the top to pivot the head and fold the ears.

30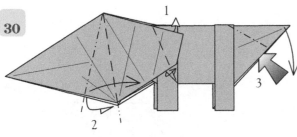

1. Fold the paper behind the ear to extend it at the top, repeat behind.
2. Crimp-fold.
3. Reverse-fold.

31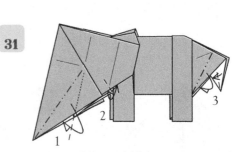

1. Reverse-fold.
2. Reverse-fold the partially hidden paper.
3. Reverse-fold.
Repeat behind.

32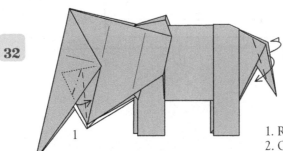

1. Reverse-fold, repeat behind.
2. Outside-reverse-fold.

33

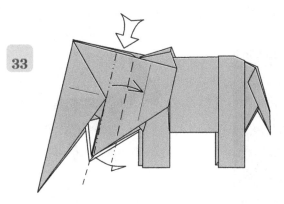

Push in at the top for this crimp fold.
Mountain-fold along the crease.

34

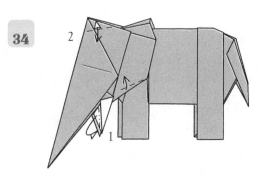

1. Fold the tusk and ear, repeat behind.
2. Fold and unfold.

35

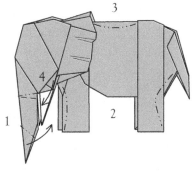

1. Sink.
2. Fold the white paper behind, repeat behind.
3. Fold inside, repeat behind.
4. Crimp-fold.

36

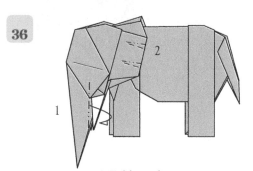

1. Fold inside.
2. Make pleat folds.
Repeat behind.

37

1. Shape the trunk with crimp and reverse folds.
2. Shape the legs, repeat behind.
3. Shape the back.
4. Curl the tusks, repeat behind.

38

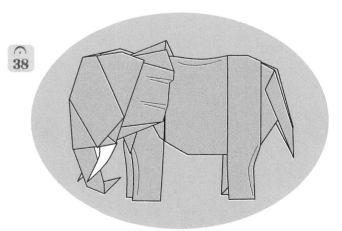

African Elephant

Donkey

Donkeys are intelligent and curious desert animals. Their large ears help them hear from far distances and also cools them down. Donkeys are strong and make good guards. For over 5,000 years, they were used as working animals, often carrying heavy cargo, and used to protect farm animals. Donkeys are social and like to be with other donkeys, horses and goats. They graze on grass and can live for 35 to 40 years.

1

Fold and unfold.

2

Fold and unfold to find the 1/4 mark.

3

Fold and unfold along the diagonal.

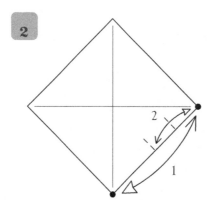

4

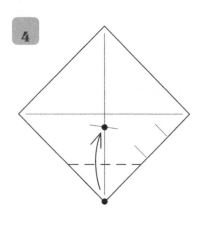

5

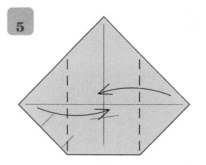

6

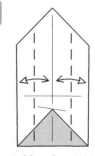

Fold and unfold the top flap.

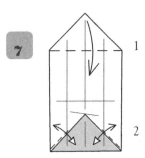

1. Fold down.
2. Fold and unfold.

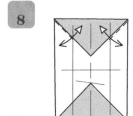

Fold and unfold.

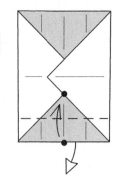

Fold up and swing out from behind.

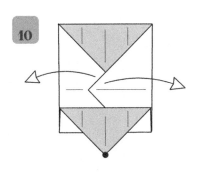

Pull out the corners. Rotate 90° so the dot goes to the right.

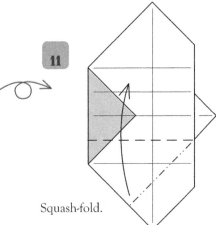

Squash-fold.

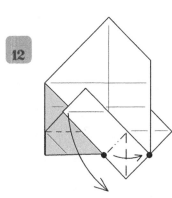

Squash-fold.

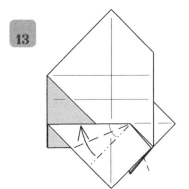

Squash-fold.

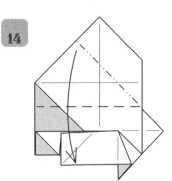

Repeat steps 11–13 on the top.

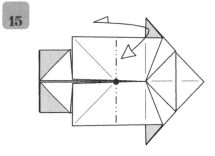

Fold and unfold.

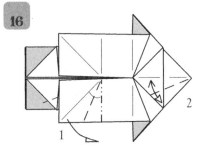

1. Squash-fold.
2. Fold and unfold.

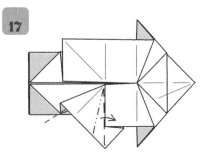

Squash-fold.

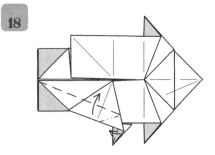

Squash-fold.

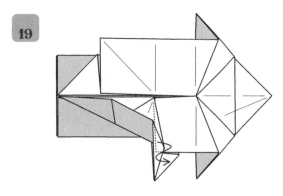

19

Tuck inside.

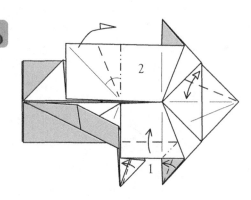

20

1. Petal-fold.
2. Repeat steps 16–20
   on the top.
Rotate 90°.

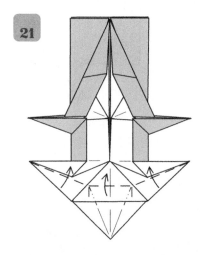

21

This is a combination
of squash folds.

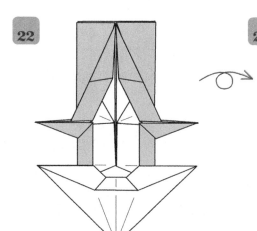

22

Rotate 180°.

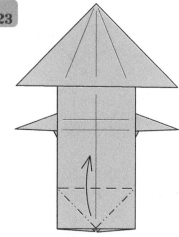

23

Petal-fold.

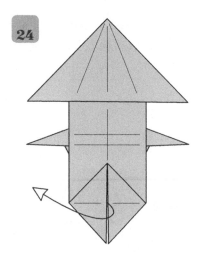

24

Pull out the hidden corner.

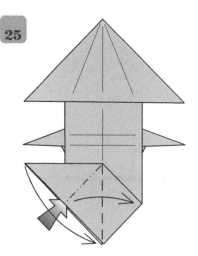

25

Squash-fold.

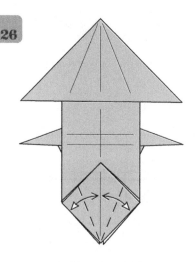

26

Fold and unfold.

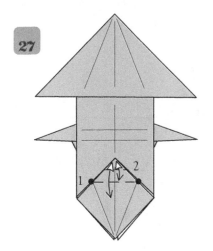

27

Fold and unfold at 1 and 2.

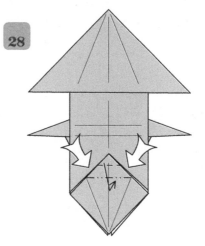

28

Sink down and up.

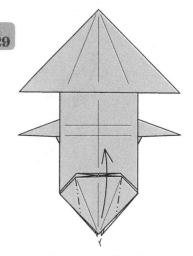

29

Begin a petal fold.

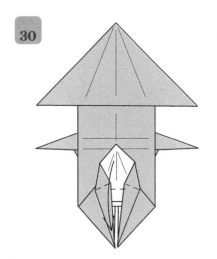

30

This is 3D. Flatten.

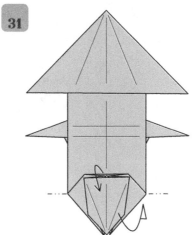

31

Wrap around
and rotate 180°.

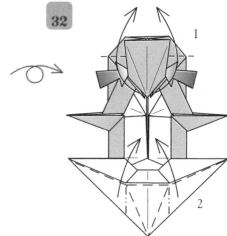

32

1. Make reverse folds.
2. This is a combination
   of squash folds.

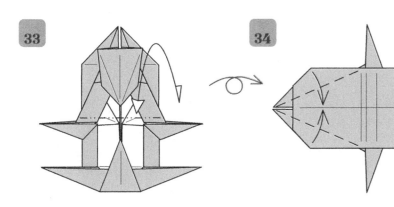

33

Fold and unfold.
Rotate 90°.

34

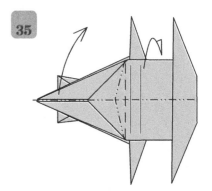

35

Fold the neck up
while folding in half.

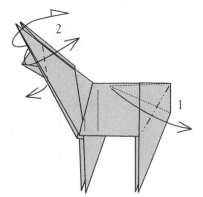

1. Reverse-fold the hidden tail.
2. Outside-reverse-fold and
   swing out the head.

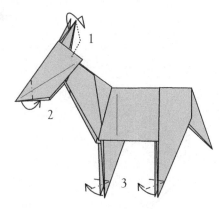

1. Pull out from behind, repeat behind.
2. Reverse-fold.
3. Make squash folds, repeat behind.

1. Fold behind, repeat behind.
2. Shape the tail.
3. Shape the legs, repeat behind.

Donkey

Indian Elephant

Slightly smaller than the African elephant, the Indian elephant reaches 9 feet tall. The highest point is on its head. Found in grasslands and tropical forests of India, China, Indonesia and elsewhere, they play a significant role in their cultures.

Begin with step 30 of the African Elephant (page 35).

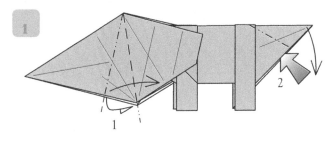

1. Crimp-fold.
2. Reverse-fold.

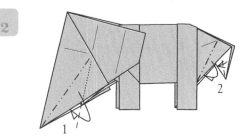

1. Reverse-fold.
2. Reverse-fold.
Repeat behind.

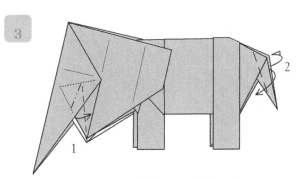

1. Reverse-fold, repeat behind.
2. Outside-reverse-fold.

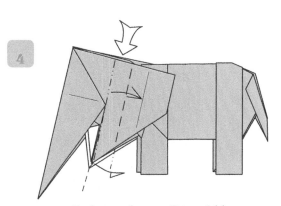

Push in at the top. Crimp-fold.
Mountain-fold along the crease.

5

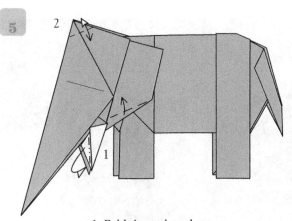

1. Fold the tusk and ear,
   repeat behind.
2. Fold and unfold.

6

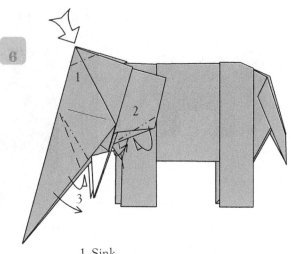

1. Sink.
2. Fold inside, repeat behind.
3. Crimp-fold.

7

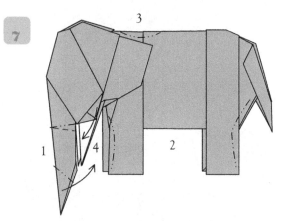

1. Shape the trunk with crimp and
   reverse folds.
2. Shape the legs, repeat behind.
3. Shape the back.
4. Curl the tusks, repeat behind.

8

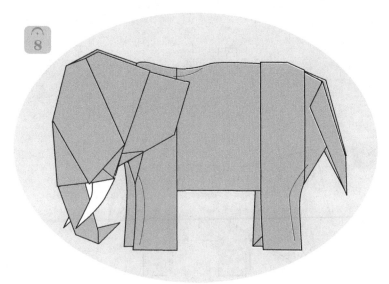

Indian Elephant

Second Movement

Andante: Animals That Bring Good Luck

A Simple Butterfly spreads its wings. Another Butterfly with antennae dances in the breeze. Swans are swimming near Goldfish and Turtles. A Crane, Cardinal and Eagle bring good luck. All swim and fly away when a Panda enters. The Panda, decorated with magnificent black and white patterns shines through and beyond this movement.

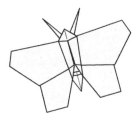

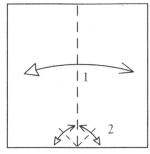

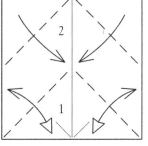

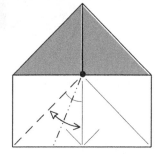

Simple Butterfly

Butterflies are graceful fliers. Since the are cold-blooded, they rely on sunlight to fly. Their four wings have colors and patterns to warn predators that they do not taste good. Butterflies cannot actually eat, as they can only drink liquids. They have taste buds on their feet. A group of butterflies is a flutter or a kaleidoscope.

1

1. Fold and unfold.
2. Fold and unfold on the bottom

2

1. Fold and unfold.
2. Fold to the center.

3

Push in at the dot to bisect the angle. Fold and unfold.

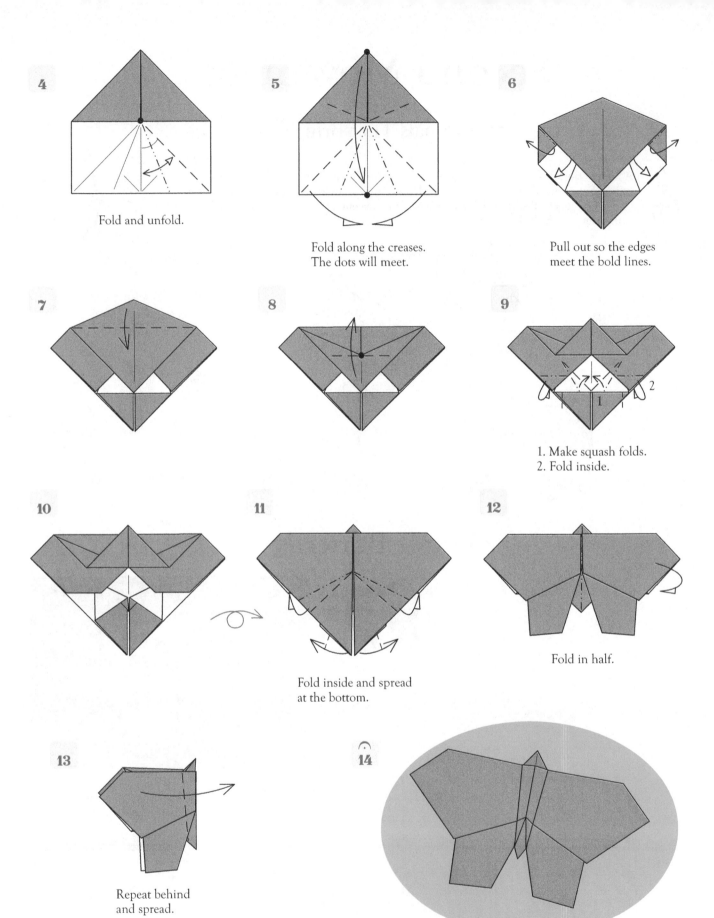

4

Fold and unfold.

5

Fold along the creases.
The dots will meet.

6

Pull out so the edges
meet the bold lines.

7

8

9

1. Make squash folds.
2. Fold inside.

10

11

Fold inside and spread
at the bottom.

12

Fold in half.

13

Repeat behind
and spread.

14

Simple Butterfly

Butterfly

In many cultures, butterflies symbolize transformation, renewal, and the fleeting nature of life. Their antennae is used to detect smell. While humans can see three colors butterflies can see nine colors, including ultraviolet. With all these colors, flowers have more colors and patterns to a butterfly, which we cannot see.

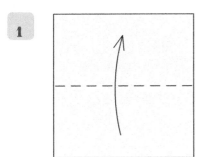

Fold in half.

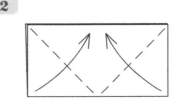

Fold and unfold.

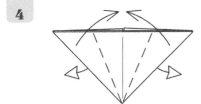

Fold to the center and swing out from behind.

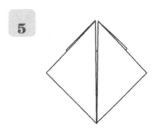

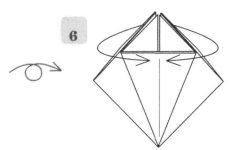

Bring the inner flap to the front.

7

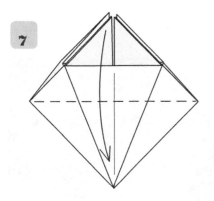

8

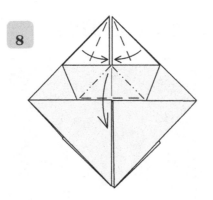

Petal-fold.

9

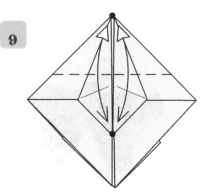

Fold and unfold.

10

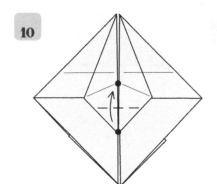

11

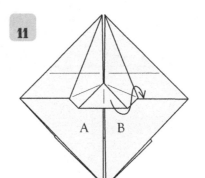

Tuck inside so triangles
A and B are on top.

12

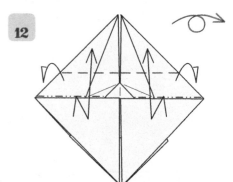

Valley-fold along the
creases for this pleat fold.

13

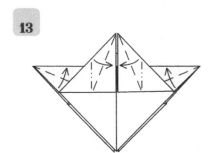

Make squash folds.

14

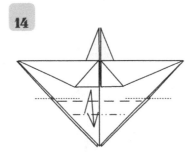

Pleat-fold. The valley line is
slightly below the hidden edge.

15

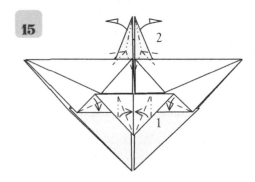

1. Make squash folds.
2. Make rabbit ears.

16

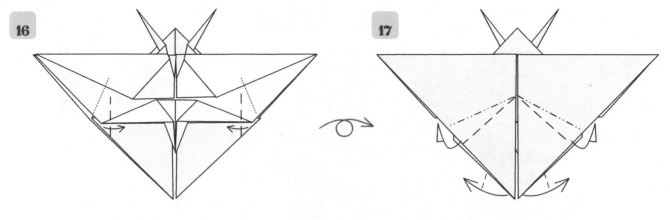

17

Fold inside and spread at the bottom.

18

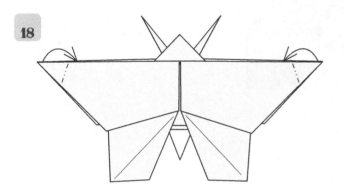

Make reverse folds.

19

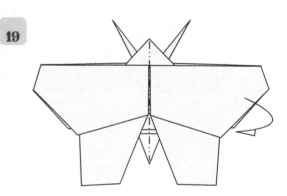

Fold in half.

20

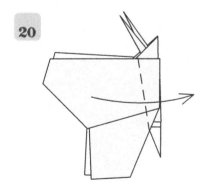

Repeat behind and spread.

21

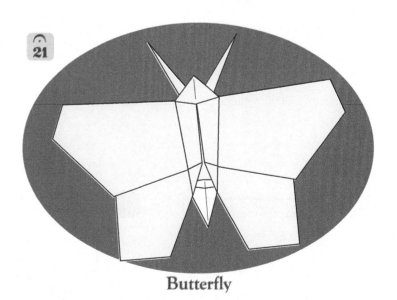

Butterfly

Goldfish

The Chinese domesticated the goldfish over 1000 years ago. A symbol of good luck, they can live for 10 to 40 years. Goldfish vary widely in size and color. They feed on plants, insects, small fish and other small creatures. They have no tongue but do have taste buds on their lips, so they check out the food before eating. Their eyes can detect ultraviolet and infrared rays so they see more colors than us. A group of goldfish is a troubling.

1

Fold in half.

2

Fold and unfold.
Repeat behind.

3

Fold and unfold
the top layer.

4

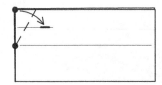

Bring the upper dot to
the line. Repeat behind.

5

Repeat behind.

6

2   1

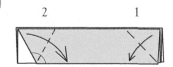

1. Fold the top flap,
   repeat behind.
2. Fold all the layers.

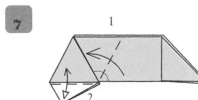

7

1. Fold all the layers.
2. Fold and unfold.

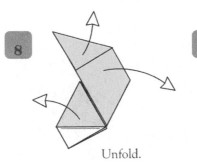

8

Unfold.

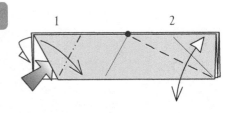

9

1. This is a combination of reverse folds on the front and back.
2. Fold and unfold, repeat behind.

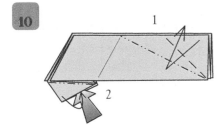

10

1. Crimp-fold, repeat behind.
2. Reverse-fold.

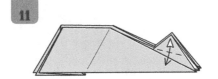

11

Fold and unfold,
repeat behind.

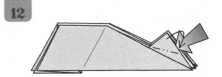

12

Reverse-fold,
repeat behind.

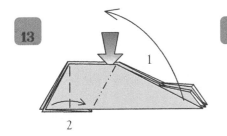

13

1. Reverse-fold.
2. Repeat behind.

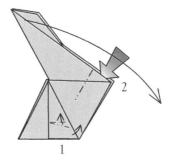

14

1. Squash-fold,
   repeat behind.
2. Reverse-fold.

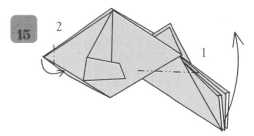

15

1. Reverse-fold all the layers.
2. Reverse-fold from the bottom.

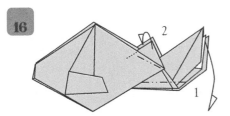

16

1. Fold the inner flap down.
2. Fold inside.
Repeat behind.

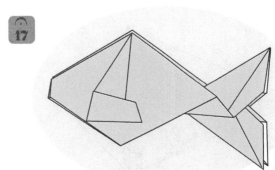

17

Goldfish

Simple Swan

As graceful swimmers, swans are a symbol of grace, beauty and peace. They feed on underwater vegetation and grasses. In flight they are called a wedge, in water they are a bevvy, and at the water's edge they are called a bank. They live up to 20 or 30 years in the wild and more in captivity.

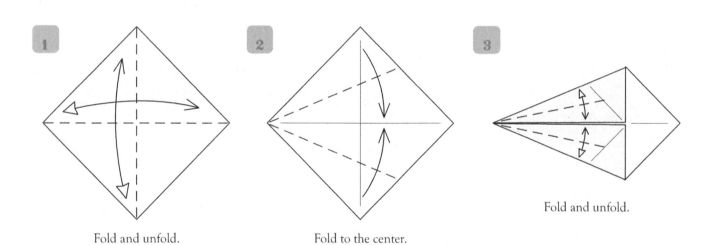

1 Fold and unfold.

2 Fold to the center.

3 Fold and unfold.

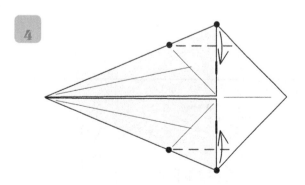

4

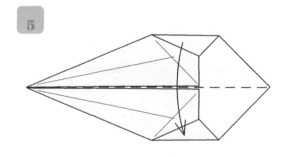

5 Fold in half.

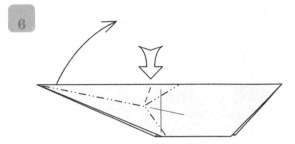

6

Double-rabbit-ear.

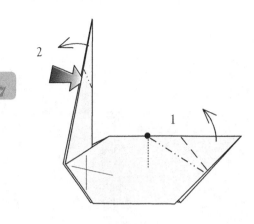

7

1. Crimp-fold.
2. Reverse-fold.

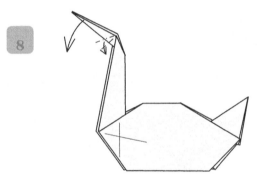

8

Outside-reverse-fold
and spread.

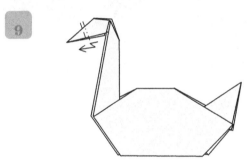

9

Crimp-fold.

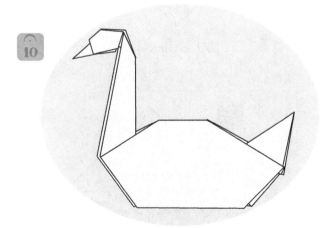

10

Simple Swan

Swan

As the largest flying bird, swans can fly for long distances and at speeds of up to 60 miles per hour. Black swans are not native to Europe but were introduced from Australia. They have webbed feet adapted for swimming.

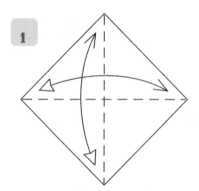

Fold and unfold.

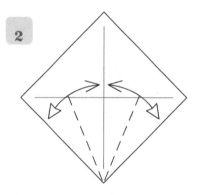

Fold and unfold.

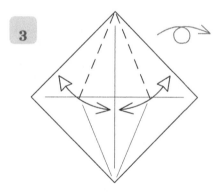

Fold and unfold.

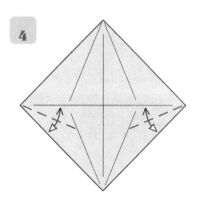

Fold and unfold.

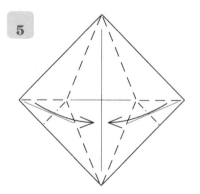

Make rabbit ears.

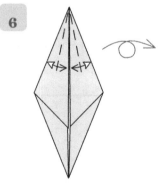

Fold and unfold.

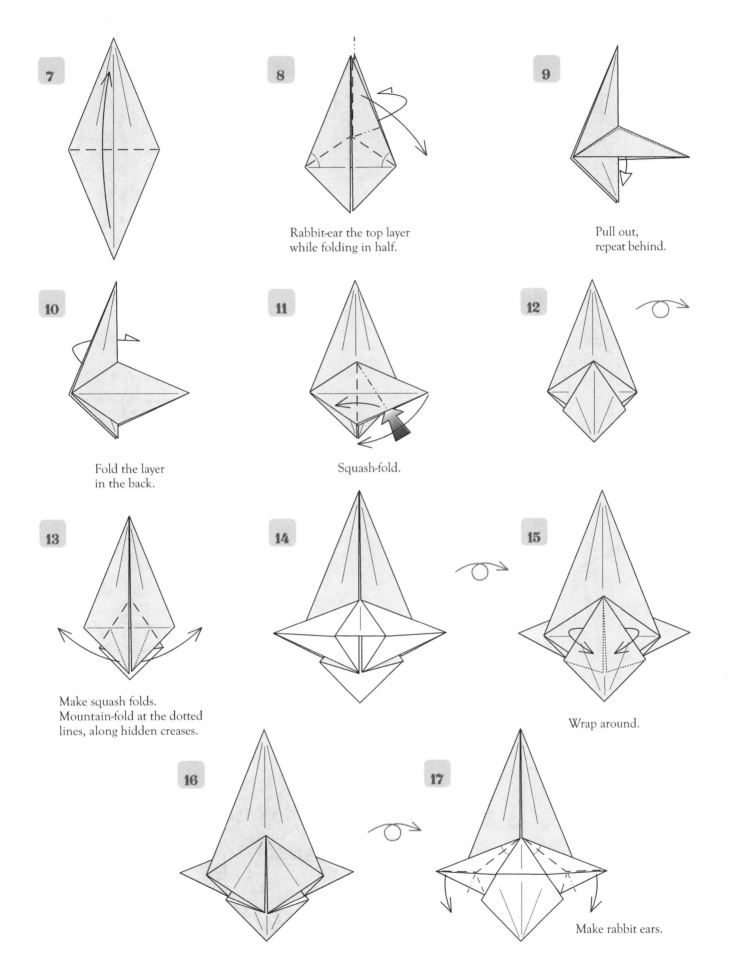

7

8

Rabbit-ear the top layer
while folding in half.

9

Pull out,
repeat behind.

10

Fold the layer
in the back.

11

Squash-fold.

12

13

Make squash folds.
Mountain-fold at the dotted
lines, along hidden creases.

14

15

Wrap around.

16

17

Make rabbit ears.

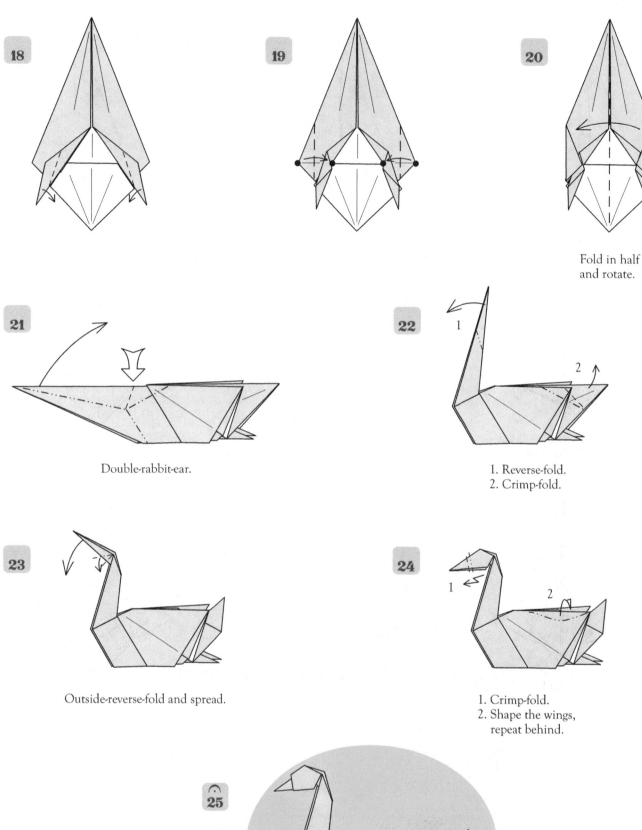

18

19

20

Fold in half and rotate.

21

Double-rabbit-ear.

22

1
2

1. Reverse-fold.
2. Crimp-fold.

23

Outside-reverse-fold and spread.

24

1
2

1. Crimp-fold.
2. Shape the wings, repeat behind.

25

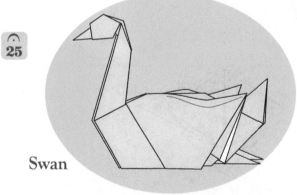

Swan

Crane

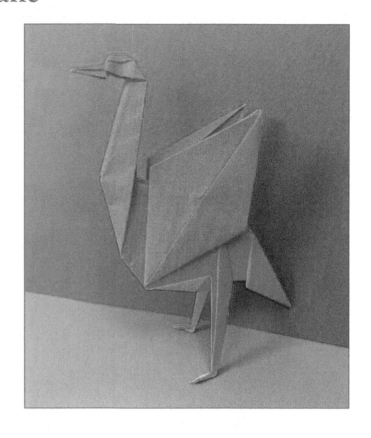

Cranes are tall birds with long legs and a long neck. These majestic, graceful and social birds fly thousands of miles every year as they migrate. As an omnivore, they feed on fish, reptiles, small mammals, insects, and plants. Growing up to six feet tall, they live for 20 to 40 years. In many cultures, cranes symbolize longevity, grace, harmony with nature, and good fortune.

1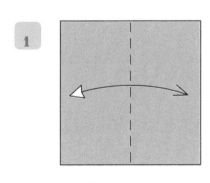

Fold and unfold.

2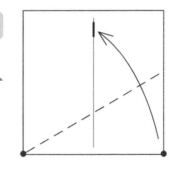

Bring the corner to the line.

3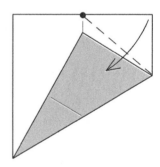

4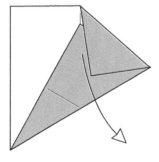

Unfold.

5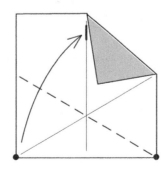

Repeat steps 2–4 in the opposite direction.

6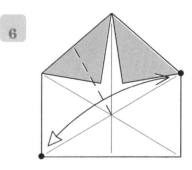

Fold and unfold.

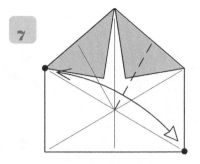

7

Fold and unfold.

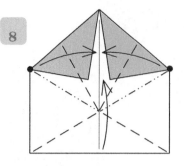

8

Fold along the creases so the dots meet.

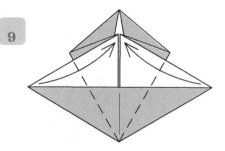

9

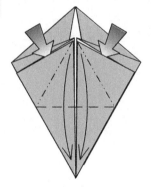

10

Make squash folds.

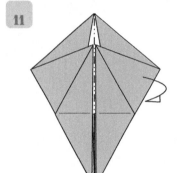

11

Fold in half and rotate.

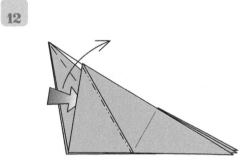

12

Reverse-fold, repeat behind.

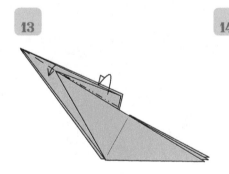

13

Reverse-fold, repeat behind.

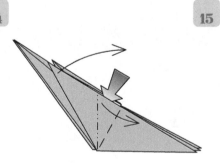

14

Squash-fold, repeat behind.

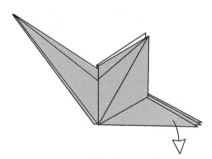

15

Slide the flap down. The fold will be adjusted in the next few steps. Repeat behind.

16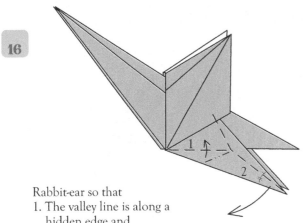

Rabbit-ear so that
1. The valley line is along a hidden edge and
2. The valley line is at an angle of 1/3 of the flap.
The fold from step 15 might need to be adjusted. Repeat behind.

17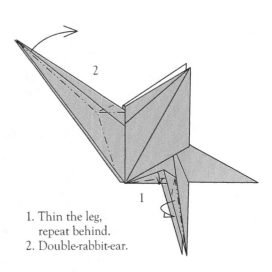

1. Thin the leg, repeat behind.
2. Double-rabbit-ear.

18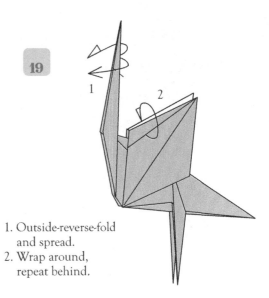

Wrap around, repeat behind.

19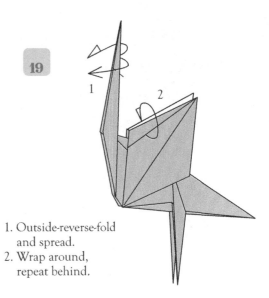

1. Outside-reverse-fold and spread.
2. Wrap around, repeat behind.

20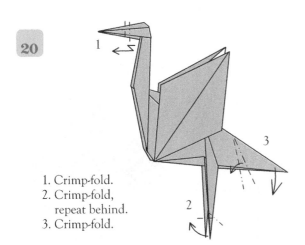

1. Crimp-fold.
2. Crimp-fold, repeat behind.
3. Crimp-fold.

21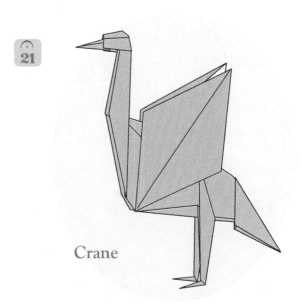

Crane

Cardinal

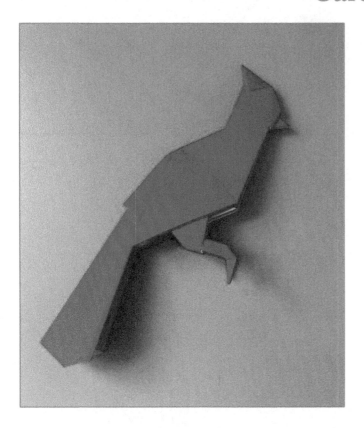

The male cardinal has vivid red feathers. The red pigment comes from their food such as red fruits or insects that fed on colorful plants. They like to forage on the ground. Cardinals are songbirds and will sing over 100 cheerful songs in the morning. We like to depict cardinals in snowy scenes.

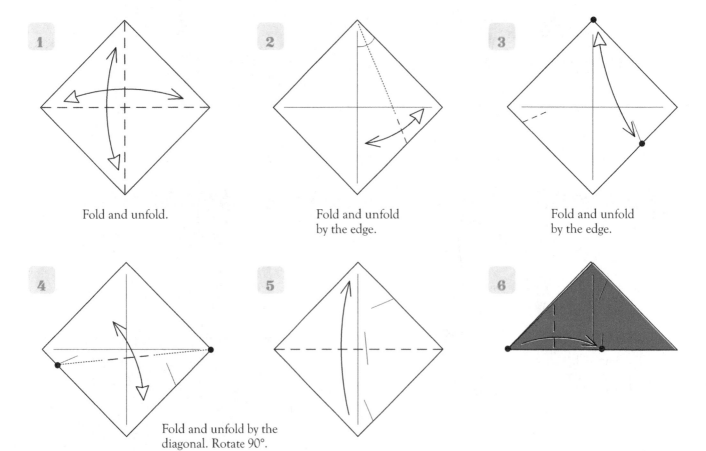

1 Fold and unfold.

2 Fold and unfold by the edge.

3 Fold and unfold by the edge.

4 Fold and unfold by the diagonal. Rotate 90°.

5

6

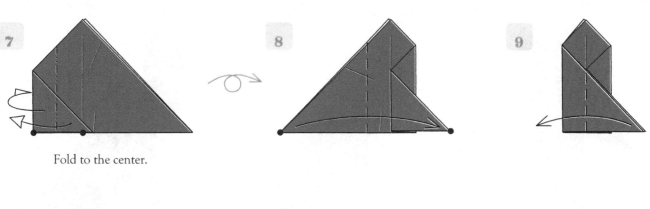

7 Fold to the center.

8

9

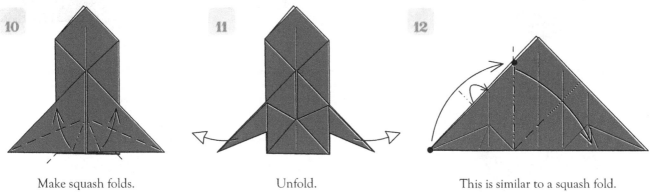

10 Make squash folds.

11 Unfold.

12 This is similar to a squash fold.

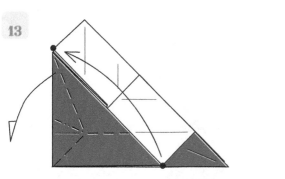
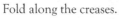

13 Fold along the creases.

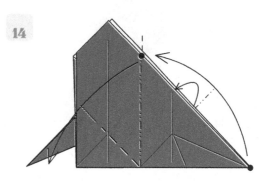

14 Repeat steps 12–13 on the right.

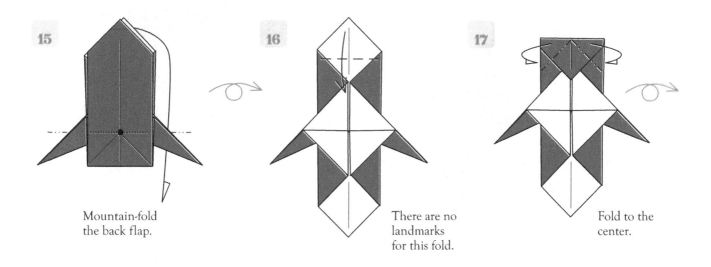

15 Mountain-fold the back flap.

16 There are no landmarks for this fold.

17 Fold to the center.

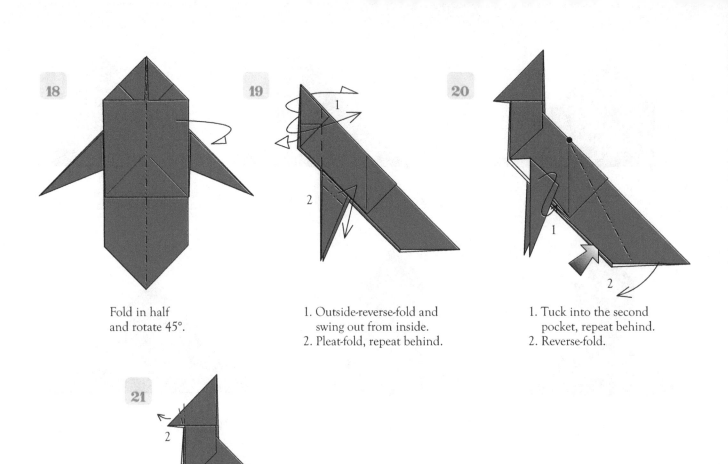

18

Fold in half
and rotate 45°.

19

1. Outside-reverse-fold and
   swing out from inside.
2. Pleat-fold, repeat behind.

20

1. Tuck into the second
   pocket, repeat behind.
2. Reverse-fold.

21

1. Fold the tail,
   repeat behind.
2. Crimp-fold.
3. Reverse-fold,
   repeat behind.

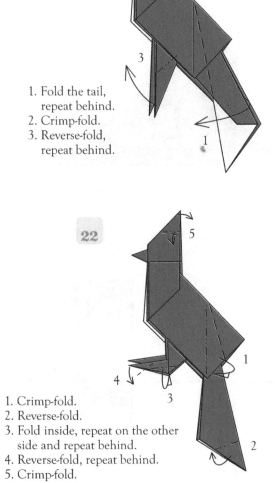

22

1. Crimp-fold.
2. Reverse-fold.
3. Fold inside, repeat on the other
   side and repeat behind.
4. Reverse-fold, repeat behind.
5. Crimp-fold.

23

Cardinal

Eagle

Eagles are large birds of prey. They are represented on several national flags as a symbol of good luck. Their large wingspan lets them fly with ease and reach altitudes above 10,000. They catch fish and small animals with their sharp talons. Eagle nests are among the largest of any bird and are found in tall trees. These intelligent birds like to play by passing sticks to each other in flight.

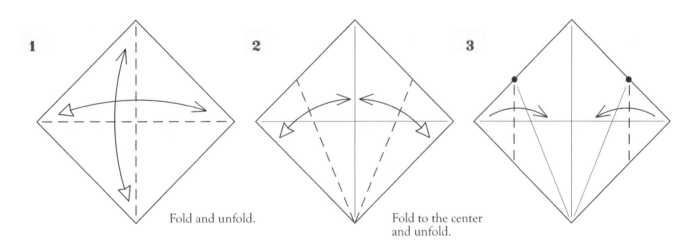

1

Fold and unfold.

2

Fold to the center and unfold.

3

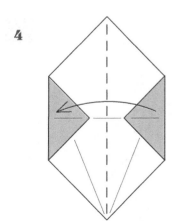

4

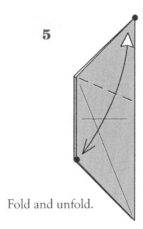

5

Fold and unfold.

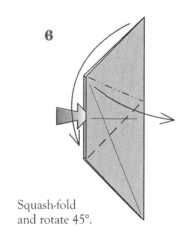

6

Squash-fold and rotate 45°.

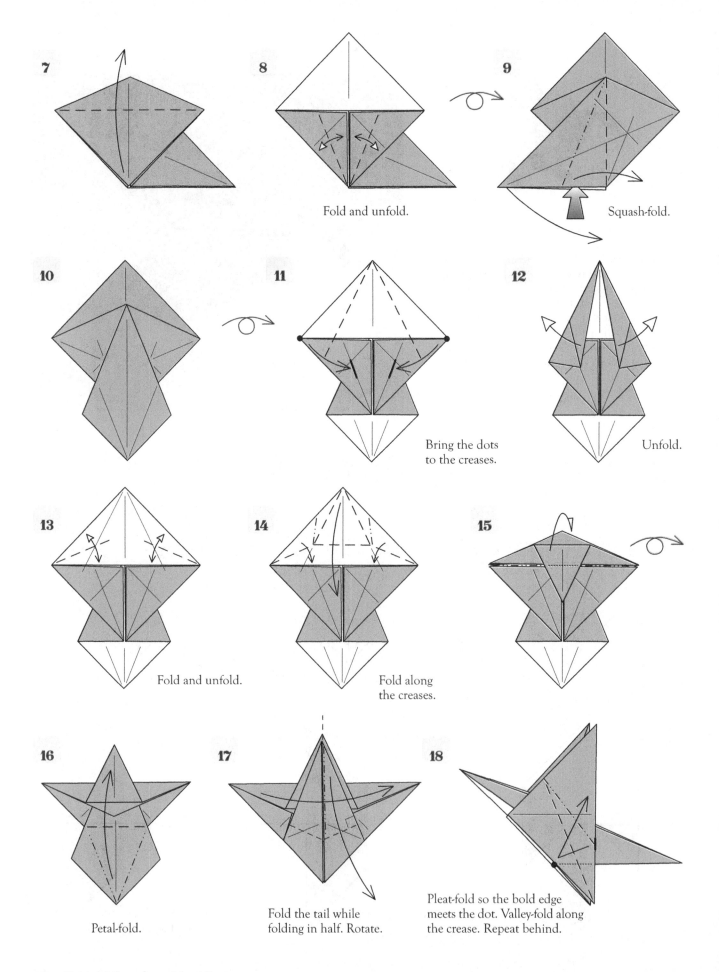

7

8

Fold and unfold.

9

Squash-fold.

10

11

Bring the dots
to the creases.

12

Unfold.

13

Fold and unfold.

14

Fold along
the creases.

15

16

Petal-fold.

17

Fold the tail while
folding in half. Rotate.

18

Pleat-fold so the bold edge
meets the dot. Valley-fold along
the crease. Repeat behind.

19

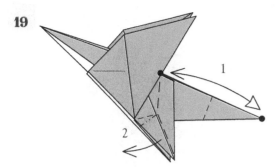

1. Fold and unfold.
2. Rabbit-ear, repeat behind.

20

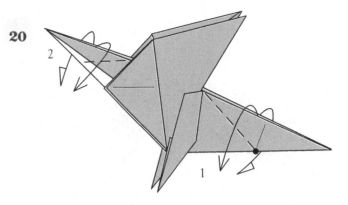

1. Outside-reverse-fold.
2. Outside-reverse-fold.

21

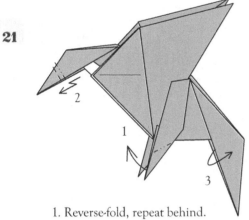

1. Reverse-fold, repeat behind.
2. Crimp-fold.
3. Pull out from inside and wrap around. Repeat behind.

22

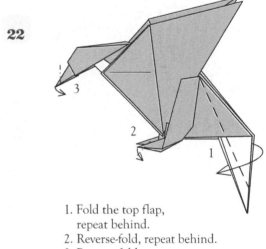

1. Fold the top flap, repeat behind.
2. Reverse-fold, repeat behind.
3. Reverse-fold.

23

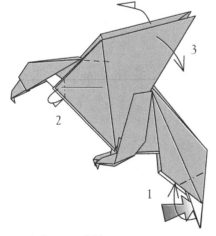

1. Reverse-fold.
2. Fold inside, repeat behind.
3. Spread the wings.
The Eagle can stand.

24

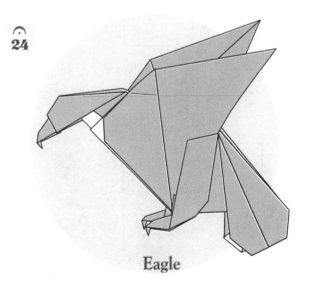

Eagle

Turtle

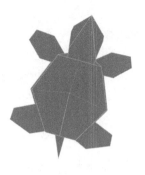

Found all over the world, turtles like to live in or near water. Turtles lived around 200 million years ago and survived the age of dinosaurs. Their shell is made from over 50 bones and continues to grow with them. Without teeth, their beak grasps their favorite foods of plants, fruits, insects, and small fish. Turtles have webbed feet while the tortoise has thick, sturdy feet. A group of turtles is a bale and a group of baby turtles is a flotilla.

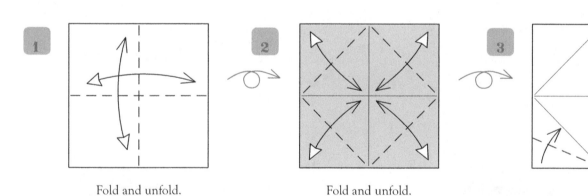

1	2	3

Fold and unfold.   Fold and unfold.

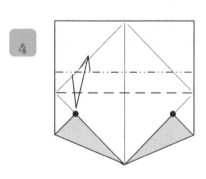

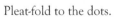

Pleat-fold to the dots.

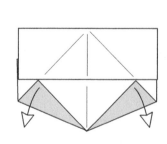

Unfold.

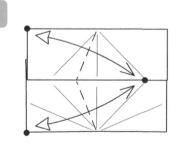

Fold and unfold.

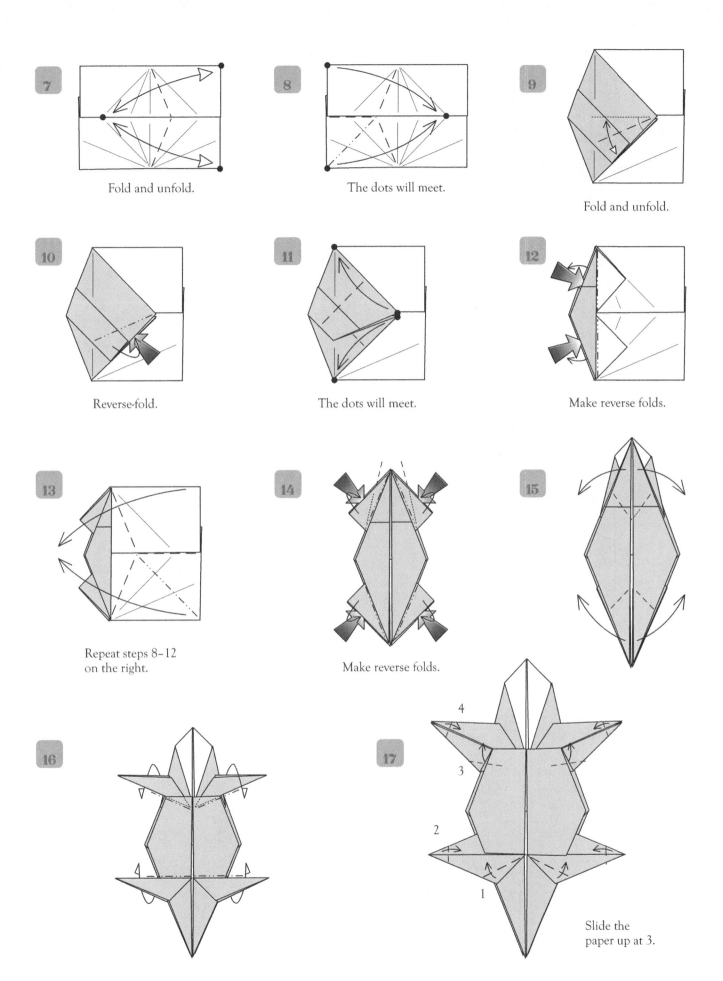

7 Fold and unfold.

8 The dots will meet.

9 Fold and unfold.

10 Reverse-fold.

11 The dots will meet.

12 Make reverse folds.

13 Repeat steps 8–12 on the right.

14 Make reverse folds.

15

16

17 Slide the paper up at 3.

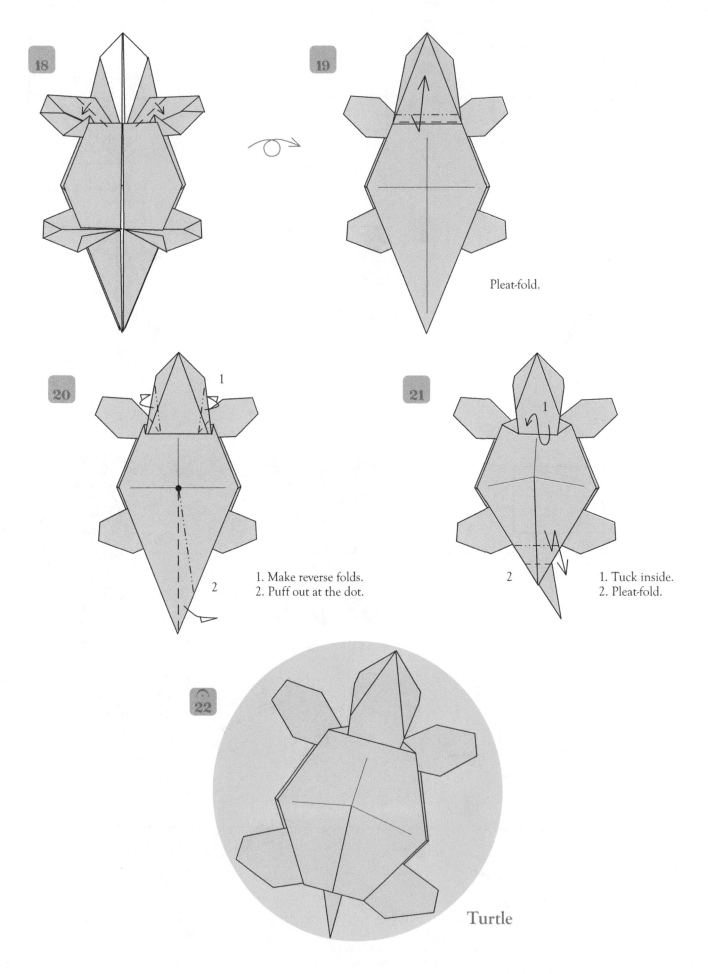

18

19

Pleat-fold.

20

1
2

1. Make reverse folds.
2. Puff out at the dot.

21

1
2

1. Tuck inside.
2. Pleat-fold.

22

Turtle

Panda

Pandas will spend 12 hours a day eating up to 100 pounds of bamboo. They also enjoy fruit and some meat. Pandas have a sixth finger that acts like a thumb, for grasping bamboo. They climb trees to avoid predators and will sleep in trees. In the wild, their lifespan is 15 to 20 years, but can live up to 30 years in captivity. When social, they will chirp, honk and bark.

1

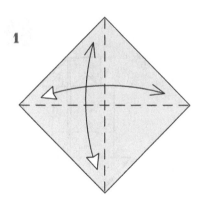

Fold and unfold.

2

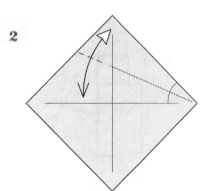

Fold and unfold on the edge.

3

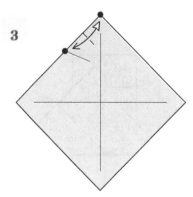

Fold and unfold on the edge.

4

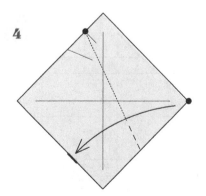

Bring the corner to the edge. Crease on the edge.

5

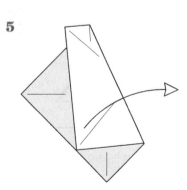

Unfold.

6

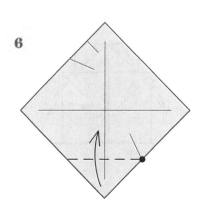

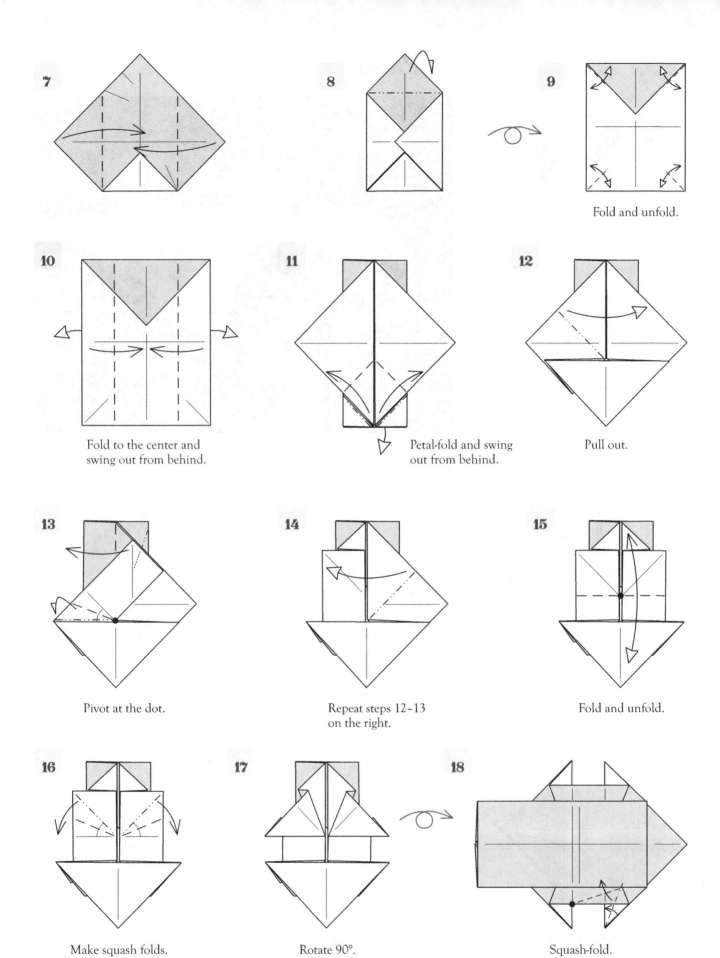

7

8

9

Fold and unfold.

10

Fold to the center and
swing out from behind.

11

Petal-fold and swing
out from behind.

12

Pull out.

13

Pivot at the dot.

14

Repeat steps 12–13
on the right.

15

Fold and unfold.

16

Make squash folds.

17

Rotate 90°.

18

Squash-fold.

19

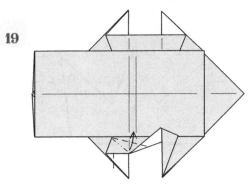

Squash-fold.

20

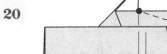
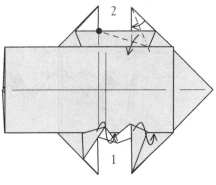

1. Tuck inside.
2. Repeat steps 18–20
   on the top.

21

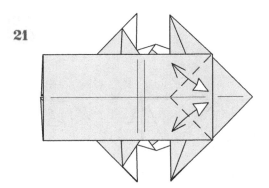

Fold and unfold the top flap.

22

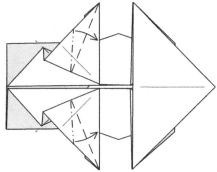

Make squash folds.

23

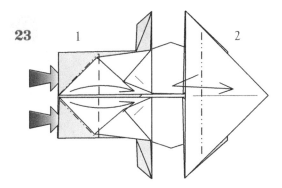

1. Make squash folds.
2. Slide the paper. This is
   similar to a pleat fold.
   Rotate 90°.

24

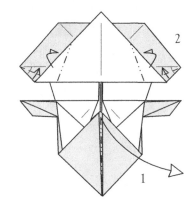

1. Pull out the corner.
2. These are similar
   to reverse folds.

25

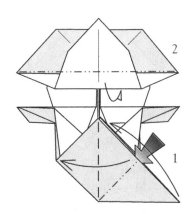

1. Squash-fold.
2. Tuck inside.

26

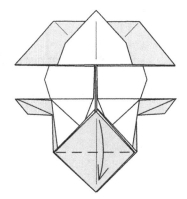

27

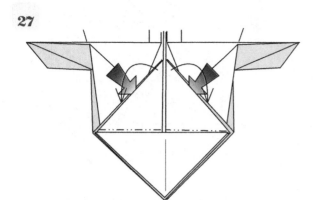

Make reverse folds.

28

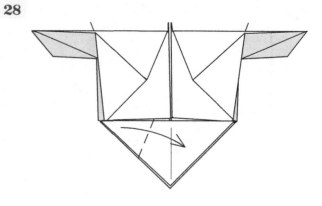

29

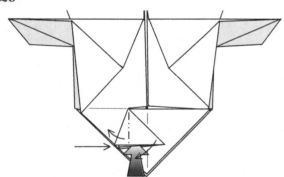

Note the horizontal line.
Open into the lower
pocket for this squash fold.

30

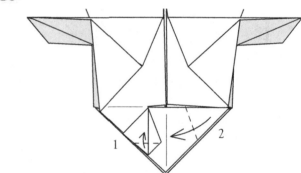

1. Fold up.
2. Repeat steps 28–30
   on the right.

31

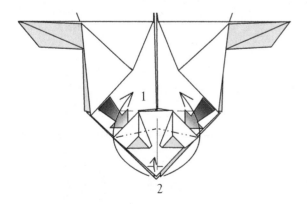

1. Make reverse folds.
2. Fold the top layer.

32

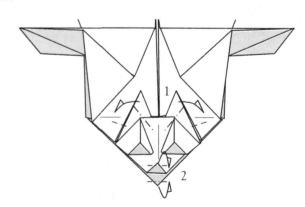

1. Pivot to form the ears.
2. Make small folds.

33

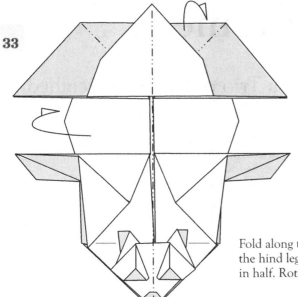

Fold along the creases by the hind legs while folding in half. Rotate 90°.

34

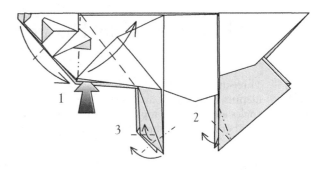

1. Squash-fold.
2. Crimp-fold, repeat behind.
3. Squash-fold, repeat behind.

35

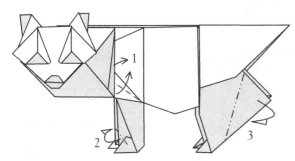

1. Spread the paper.
2. Fold behind, repeat behind.
3. Fold behind, repeat behind.

36

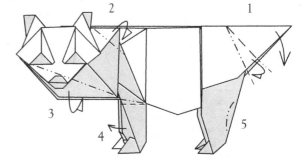

1. Crimp-fold.
2. Fold inside.
3. Tuck inside, repeat behind.
4. Pleat-fold, repeat behind.
5. Shape the leg, repeat behind.

37

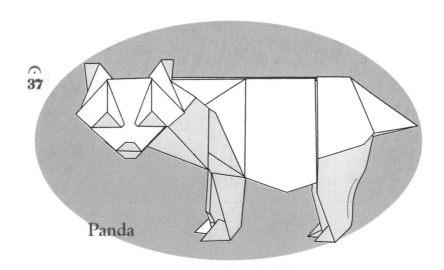

Panda

Third Movement

Minuet of Lucky Diamonds with a Trio of Colorful Octahedra

Three-dimensional diamonds show the geometric side of origami. Each diamond is composed of identical pyramids joined at the base. The faces are identical isosceles triangles with varying apex angles (angles at the top). For these lucky diamonds, the apex angle is 180/(n - 1), where n is the number of sides of the polygon base. This collection ranges from triangular to nonagonal diamonds.

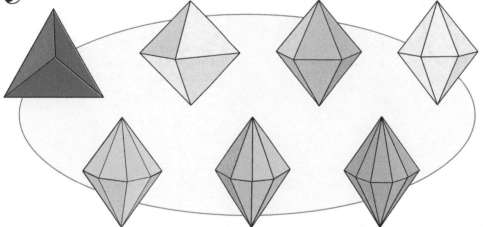

Diamond	Apex Angle
Triangular	90°
Square	60°
Pentagonal	45°
Hexagonal	36°
Heptagonal	30°
Octagonal	25.7°
Nonagonal	22.5°

Triangular Dipyramid

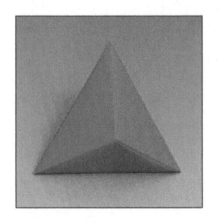

The angles of each of the six triangles are 90°, 45°, and 45°. The layout show 3/4 symmetry.

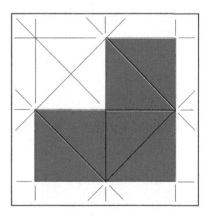

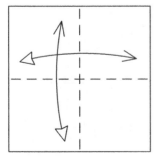

1

Fold and unfold.

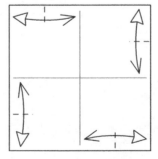

2

Fold and unfold to find the quarter mark on each side.

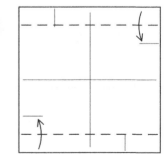

3

Rotate 90°.

4

5

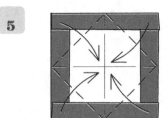

Fold to the center.

6

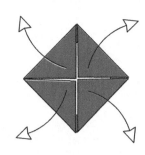

Unfold everything.

7

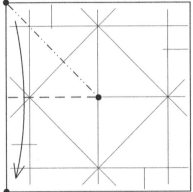

Push in at the center dot. The other two dots will meet.

8

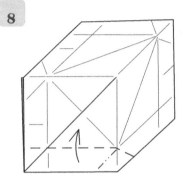

Fold along the creases.

9

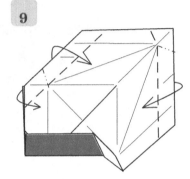

Fold along the creases.

10

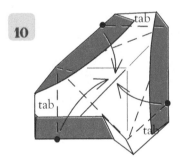

tab

tab

tab

Bring the dots together. The tabs will lock the model.

11

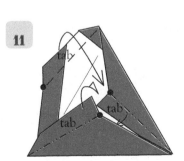

tab

tab

tab

The fold is in progress. Bring the three dots together and close the model with a three-way twist lock.

12

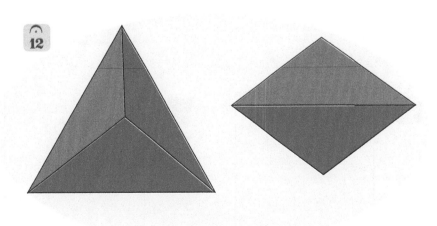

Triangular Dipyramid

Octahedron

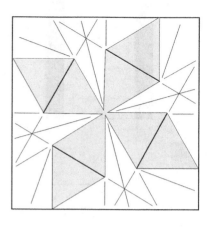

The octahedron is composed of eight equilateral triangles. It can be used as a base to create more polyhedra. According to Plato, the octahedron represented air because it appears to be suspended.

This model uses square symmetry and closes with a four-way twist lock.

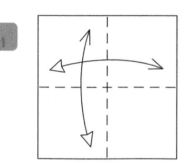

Fold and unfold.

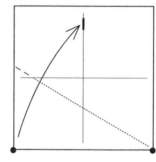

Bring the left dot to the line. Crease on the left.

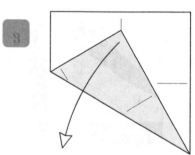

Unfold and rotate 90°.

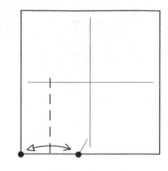

Fold and unfold.

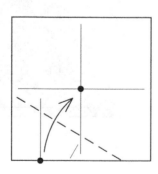

1. Fold and unfold along the edge.
2. Unfold.

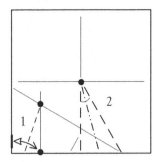

1. Bring the edge to the dot and unfold.
2. Fold and unfold to bisect the angle. It is easier to turn the paper over.

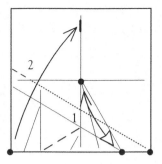

1. Fold and unfold.
2. Repeat steps 2–8 three times.

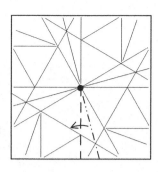

Fold along the creases and push in at the dot.

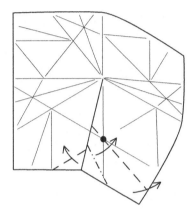

Squash-fold and flatten. Valley-fold along the creases. Rotate 90°.

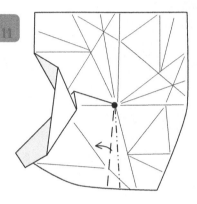

Repeat steps 9–10 three times. Rotate to view the outside.

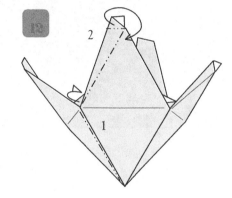

1. Fold and unfold.
2. Wrap all around. Repeat all around.

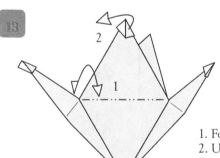

1. Fold and unfold.
2. Unfold.
Repeat all around.

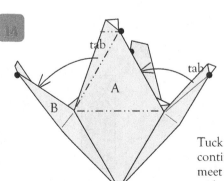

Tuck the tabs under A and B and continue all around. The dots will meet at the top. The model closes with a four-way twist lock.

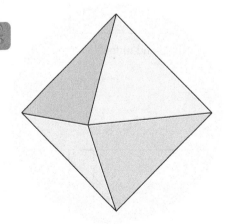

Octahedron

Pentagonal Dipyramid

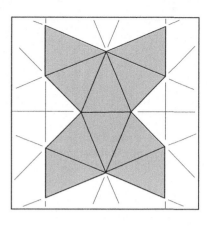

The angles of each of the ten triangles are 45°, 67.5°, and 67.5°.

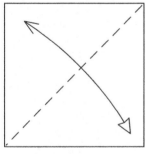

Fold and unfold.

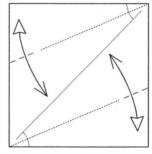

Fold and unfold along the edges.

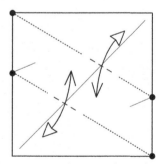

Fold and unfold on the diagonal.

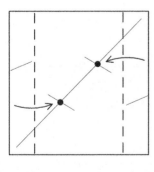

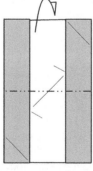

Fold in half.

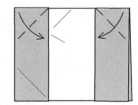

7

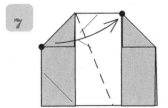

8

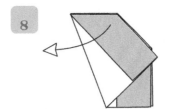

Unfold.

9

Fold and unfold.

10

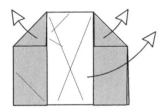

Unfold everything.

11

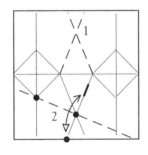

1. Fold and unfold along the creases.
2. Fold and unfold.

12

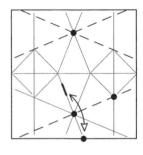

Fold and unfold
three times.

13

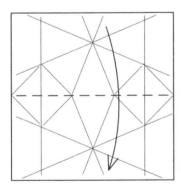

14

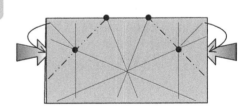

Make reverse folds along
the creases by the dots.

15

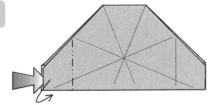

Reverse-fold. Turn
over and repeat.

16

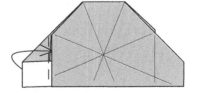

Tuck inside. Turn
over and repeat.

Pentagonal Dipyramid **81**

Puff out at the dot and
fold along the creases.
Turn over and repeat.

18

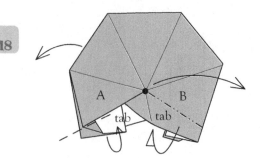

Bring the dot to the right and the
one behind to the left. Follow
regions A and B into the next step.
Fold all the layers of each tab.

19

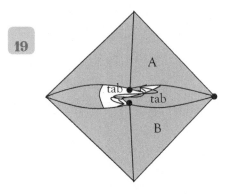

Tuck the two tabs into each
other so the center dots meet.

20

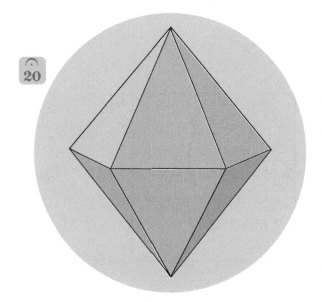

Pentagonal Dipyramid

Hexagonal Dipyramid

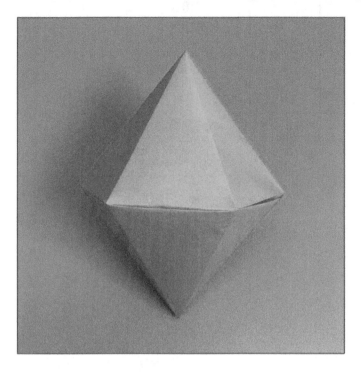

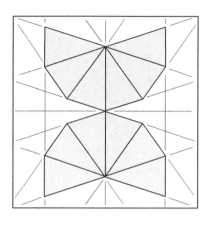

The angles of each of the twelve triangles are 36°, 72°, and 72°.

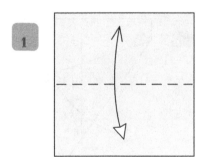

1 Fold and unfold.

2 Fold and unfold by the right.

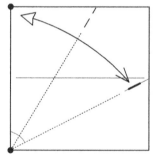

3 Fold and unfold on the top to bisect the angle.

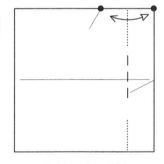

4 Fold and unfold in the center.

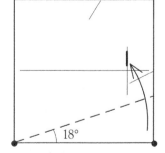

5 Bring the corner to the crease. The 18° angle is exact.

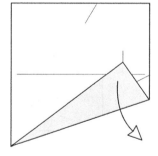

6 Unfold.

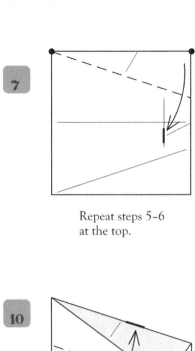

7

Repeat steps 5–6
at the top.

8

Fold and unfold.

9

1. Fold along the crease.
2. Valley-fold.

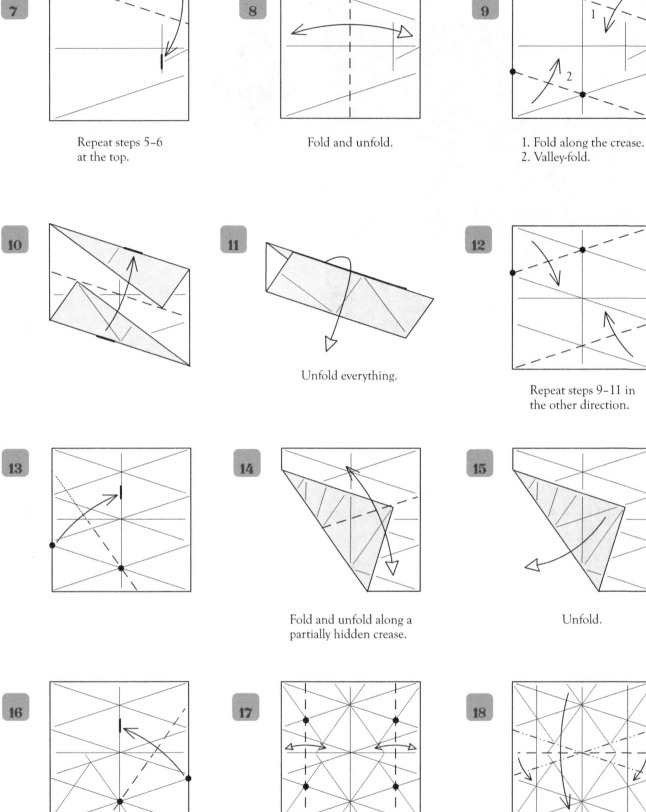

10

11

Unfold everything.

12

Repeat steps 9–11 in
the other direction.

13

14

Fold and unfold along a
partially hidden crease.

15

Unfold.

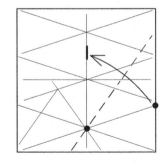

16

Repeat steps 13–15
three times, on the
right and at the top.

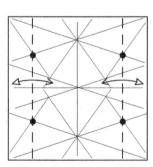

17

Fold and unfold.

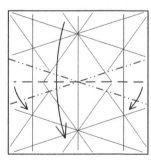

18

Fold along the creases.

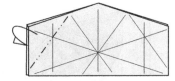

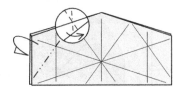

Inside view. Fold the inside layers together for this spine-lock fold. Turn over and repeat.

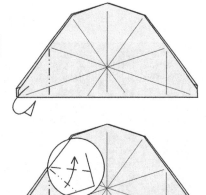

Inside view. Fold the inside layers together for this spine-lock fold. Turn over and repeat.

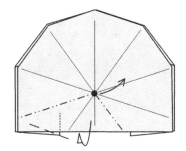

Puff out at the dot and fold along the creases. Turn over and repeat.

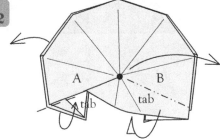

Bring the dot to the right and the one behind to the left. Follow regions A and B into the next step. Fold all the layers of each tab.

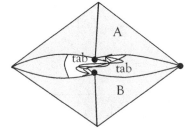

Tuck the two tabs into each other so the center dots meet.

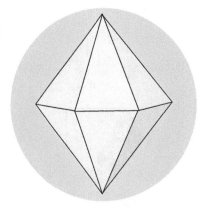

Hexagonal Dipyramid

Heptagonal Dipyramid

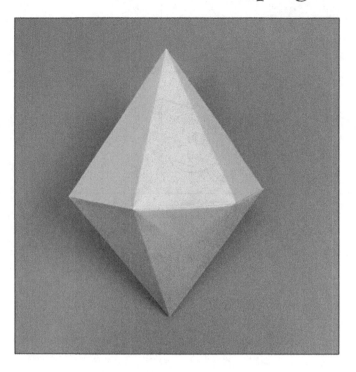

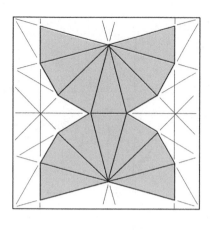

The angles of each of the twelve triangles are 30°, 75°, and 75°.

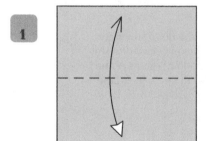

Fold and unfold.

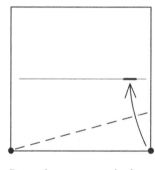

Bring the corner to the line.

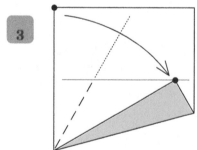

Fold on the lower half.

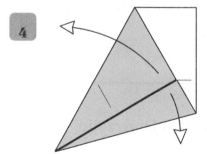

Unfold.

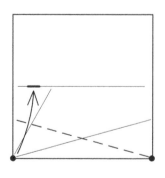

Repeat steps 2–4 in the other direction. Rotate 180°.

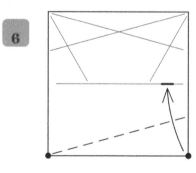

Repeat steps 2–5.

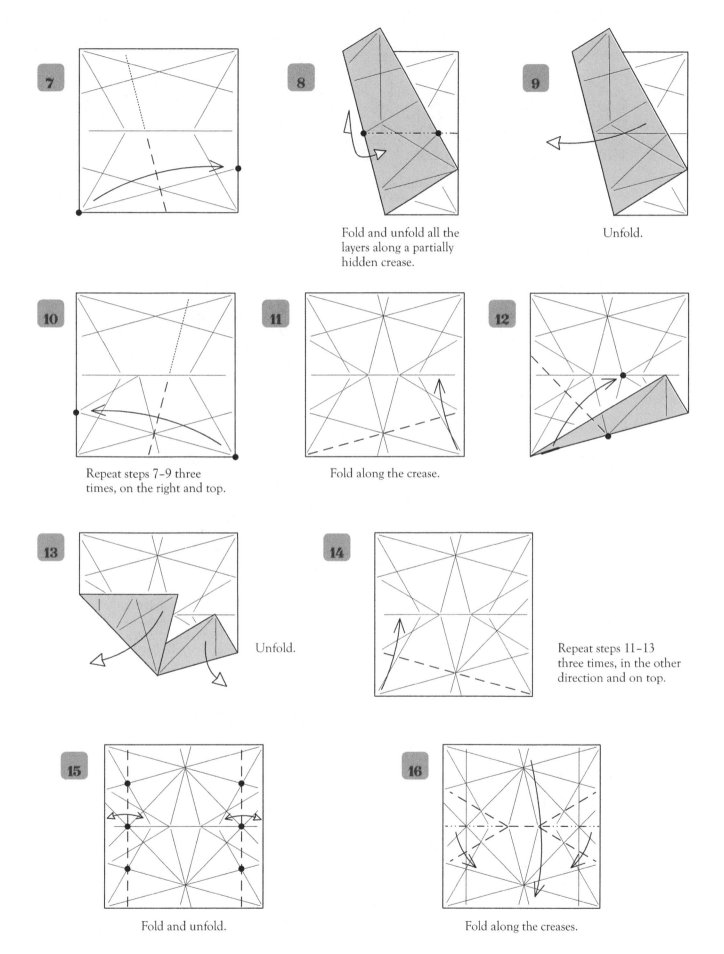

7

8 Fold and unfold all the layers along a partially hidden crease.

9 Unfold.

10 Repeat steps 7–9 three times, on the right and top.

11 Fold along the crease.

12

13 Unfold.

14 Repeat steps 11–13 three times, in the other direction and on top.

15 Fold and unfold.

16 Fold along the creases.

17

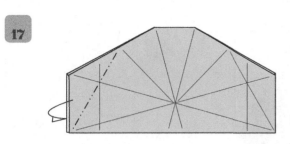 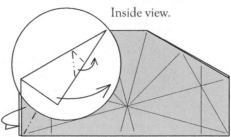

Inside view.

Fold the layers together at the dot for this
spine-lock fold. Turn over and repeat.

18

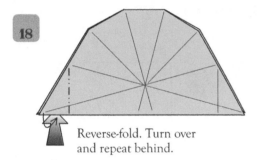

Reverse-fold. Turn over
and repeat behind.

19

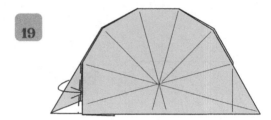

Tuck inside. Turn over
and repeat behind.

20

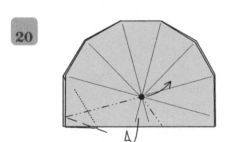

Puff out at the dot and
fold along the creases.
Turn over and repeat.

21

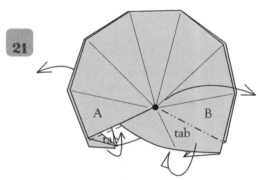

Bring the dot to the right and the
one behind to the left. Follow
regions A and B into the next step.
Fold all the layers of each tab.

22

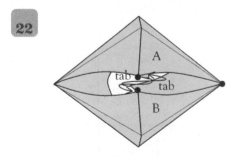

Tuck the two tabs into each
other so the center dots meet.

23

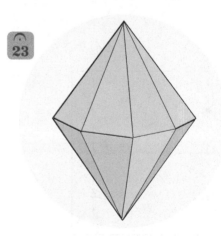

Heptagonal Dipyramid

Octagonal Dipyramid

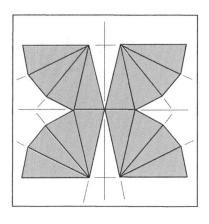

The angles of each of the sixteen triangles are 25.7°, 77.1°, and 77.1°. These angles makes the geometry convenient since the horizontal lines are part of the crease pattern.

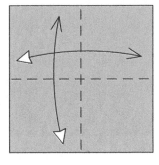

Fold and unfold.

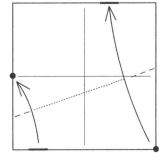

Bring the lower right corner to the top edge and the bottom edge to the left center. Crease on the left and right.

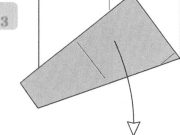

Unfold.

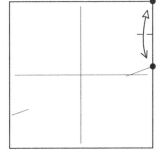

Fold and unfold on the right.

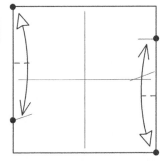

Fold and unfold on the edges. Rotate 90°.

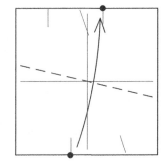

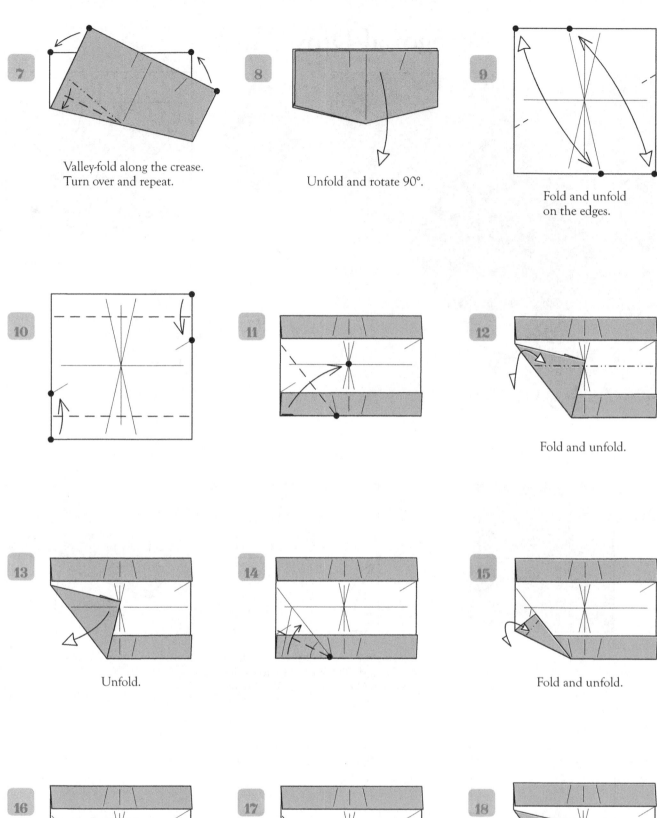

7

Valley-fold along the crease.
Turn over and repeat.

8

Unfold and rotate 90°.

9

Fold and unfold
on the edges.

10

11

12

Fold and unfold.

13

Unfold.

14

15

Fold and unfold.

16

Unfold.

17

Fold along the crease.

18

Fold and unfold
along the creases.

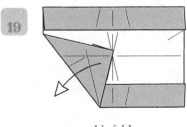

19

Unfold.

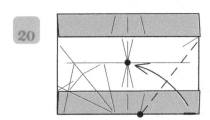

20

Repeat steps 11–19 three times, on the right and at the top.

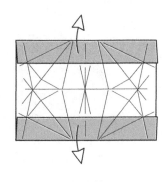

21

Unfold.

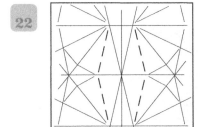

22

Fold and unfold along the creases.

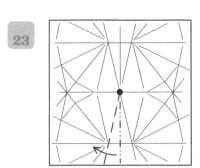

23

Push in at the dot.

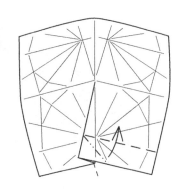

24

Squash-fold and rotate 180°.

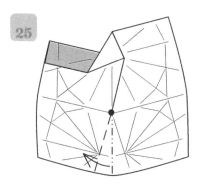

25

Repeat steps 23–24. Then flatten.

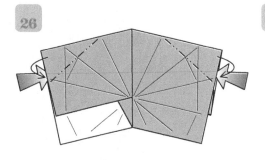

26

Make reverse folds.

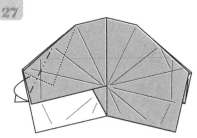

27

Fold the inside layers together for this spine-lock fold. Turn over and repeat.

28

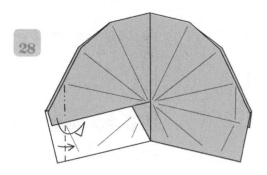

Fold the inside layers together for this spine-lock fold. Turn over and repeat.

29

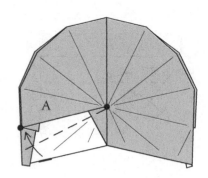

Bring the edge to the dot. All of the folds will be under region A. Turn over and repeat.

30

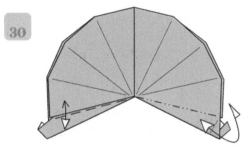

Fold and unfold.

31

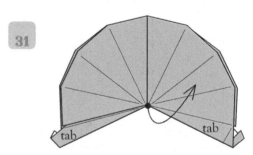

Lift up at the dot to open the model. Tuck and interlock the tabs.

32

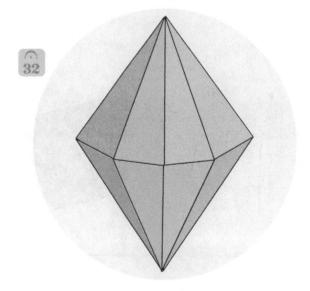

Octagonal Dipyramid

Nonagonal Dipyramid

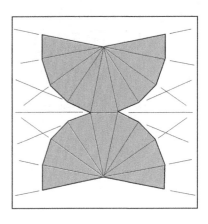

The angle at the top of the triangle in this 18-sided dipyramid is 22.5°. The other two angles are both 78.75°.

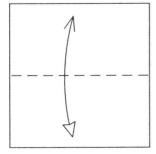

Fold and unfold.

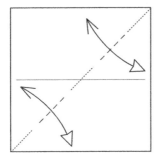

Fold and unfold along the diagonal.

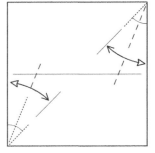

Fold and unfold on the center line.

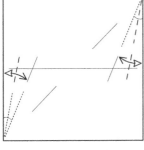

Fold and unfold on the center line.

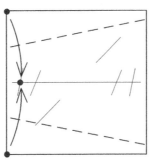

The dots will meet.

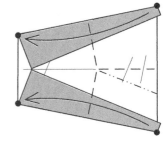

This is similar to a rabbit ear. The dots will meet.

7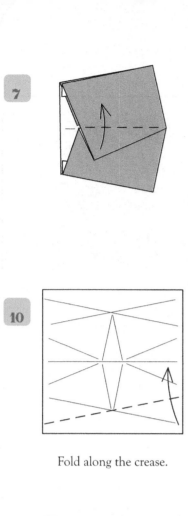

8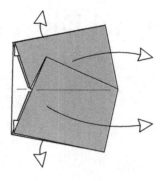

Unfold everything
and rotate 180°.

9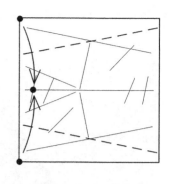

Repeat steps 5–8.

10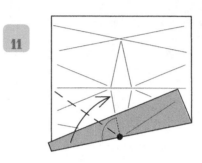

Fold along the crease.

11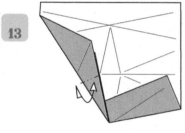

12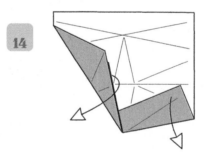

Fold along the crease.

13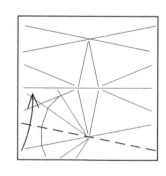

Fold and unfold along
a hidden crease.

14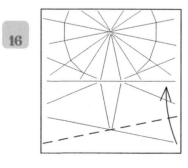

Unfold everything.

15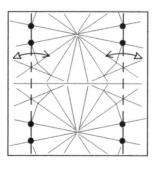

Repeat steps 10–14 in
the opposite direction.
Rotate 180°.

16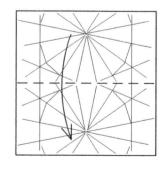

Repeat steps 10–15.

17

Fold and unfold along
creases at the dots.

18

Fold in half.

19

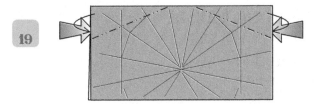

Make revese folds
along the creases.

20

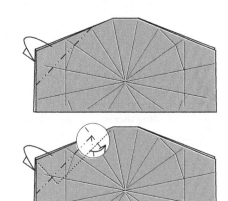

Inside view. Fold the inside layers
together for this spine-lock fold.
Turn over and repeat.

21

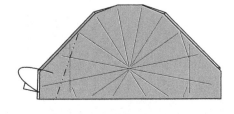

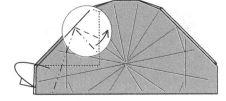

Inside view. Fold the inside layers
together for this spine-lock fold.
Turn over and repeat.

22

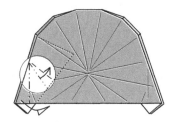

Inside view. Fold the inside layers
together for this spine-lock fold.
Turn over and repeat.

23

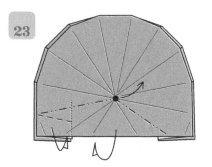

Puff out at the dot and fold
along the creases. Valley-fold
along an inner flap. Turn
over and repeat.

24

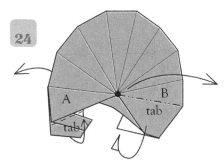

Bring the dot to the right
and the one behind to the
left. Follow regions A and
B into the next step. Fold
all the layers of each tab.

25

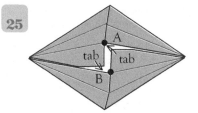

Tuck the two tabs inside
to lock the model. The
dots will meet.

26

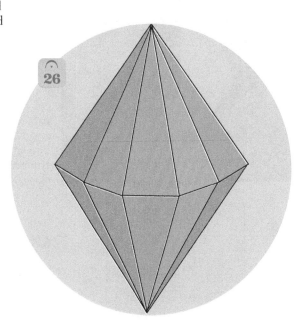

Nonagonal Dipyramid

Trio of Shapes Based on Cubes

One of the Lucky Diamonds is the Octahedron. Here is a trio of octahedra with fun color-change patterns. Each of these models uses square symmetry so the crease pattern is the same when rotated 90°, which simplifies the folding method. These colorful octahedra add magic to origami.

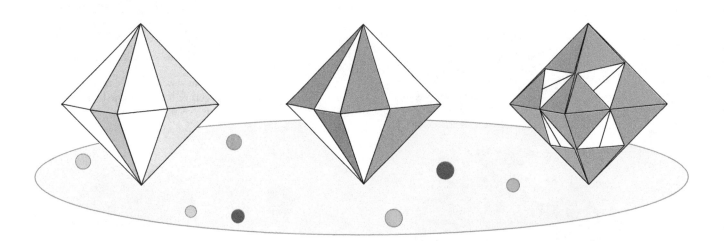

Marble Octahedron

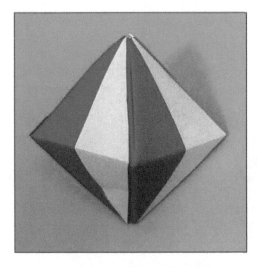

This marble octahedron has two colors on each face. The color pattern is made from the base in step 11, which is then formed into an octahedron. Square symmetry is used and the model closes with a four-way twist lock.

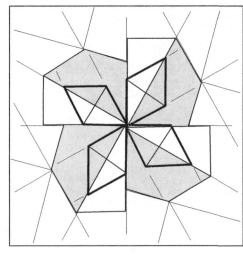

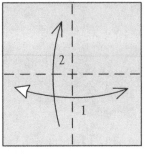

Fold and unfold.

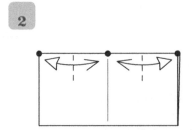

Fold and unfold.

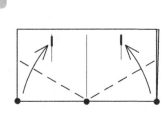

Bring the corners to the lines.

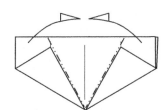

Fold to the center.

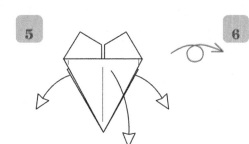

Unfold.

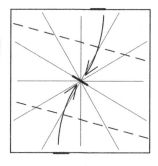

Bring the edges to the line.

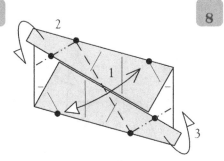

1. Fold and unfold.
2,3. Fold along the creases between the dots.

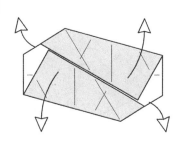

Unfold and rotate 90°.

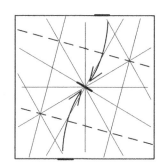

Repeat steps 6–7.

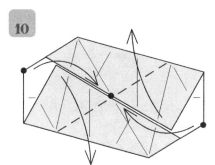

Fold along the creases and bring the outer dots to the center.

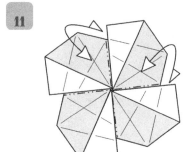

Fold and unfold.

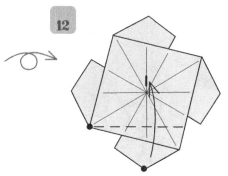

Bring the dot to the line.

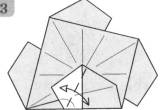

Fold and unfold.

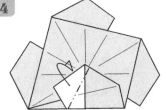

Fold behind along the crease.

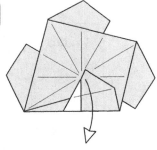

Unfold.

Marble Octahedron **97**

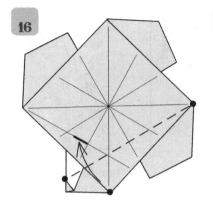

16

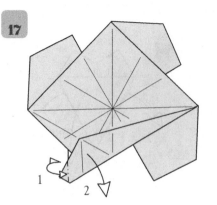

17

1. Fold and unfold.
2. Unfold.
Rotate.

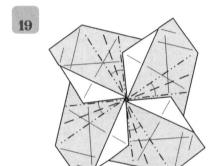

18

Repeat steps 12–17
three times.

19

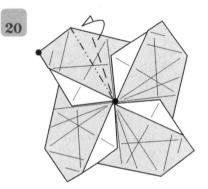

20

Fold and unfold to
bisect the angle.

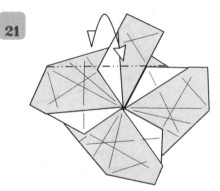

21

Puff out at the center dot.
Rotate so the dot on the
left goes to the top.

Fold and unfold along
the creases. Rotate 90°.

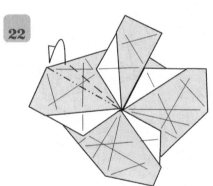

22

Repeat steps 20–21
three times.

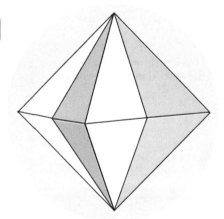

24

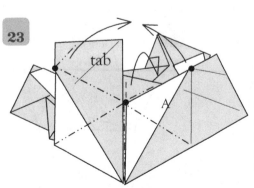

23

tab

A

The model closes with a four-
way twist lock. One of our sides
is shown. Puff out at the lower
dot, the upper dots will meet
and A will cover the tab.

Marble Octahedron

Kaleidoscopic Octahedron

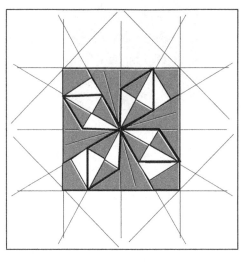

Each of the eight faces of this octahedron has two color-change triangles that alternate on all sides. This model uses square symmetry and closes with a four-way twist lock.

1

Fold and unfold.

2

Fold to the center and unfold.

3

4

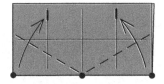

Bring the corners to the lines.

5

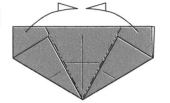

Fold to the center.

6

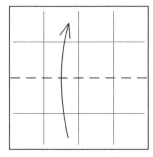

Unfold.

7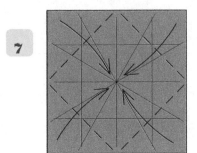

Fold to the center.

8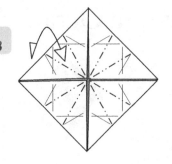

Fold and unfold along
the hidden creases.

9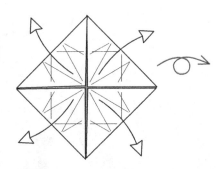

Unfold.

10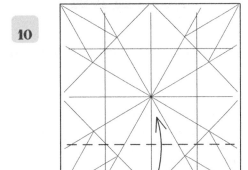

Fold along the crease.

11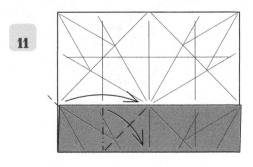

Squash-fold along the creases.

12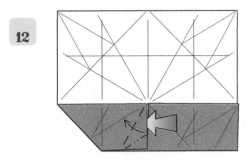

Valley-fold along the crease
for this squash fold.

13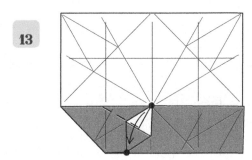

14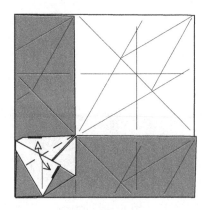

Reverse-fold.

15

Fold and unfold.

16

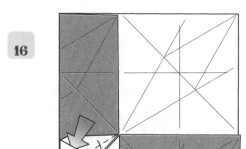

Reverse-fold and rotate 90°.

17

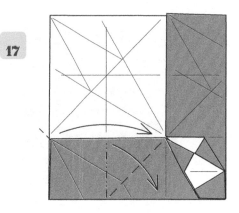

Repeat steps 11–16
three times.

18

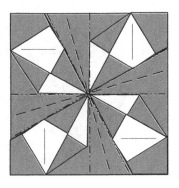

Fold and unfold to
bisect the angle.

19

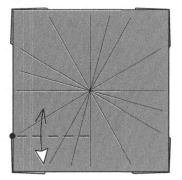

Fold and unfold.

20

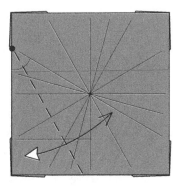

Fold and unfold.

21

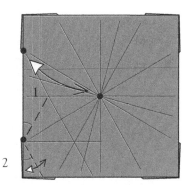

Fold and unfold at 1 and 2. The
two angles by the lower dot are
about the same. Rotate 90°.

22

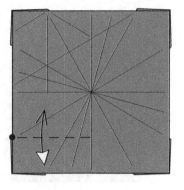

Repeat steps 19–21
three times.

23

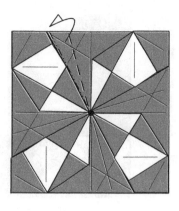

Puff out at the dot.

24

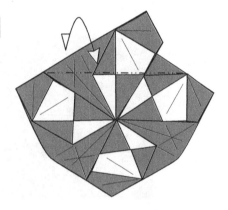

Fold and unfold along
the creases. Rotate 90°.

25

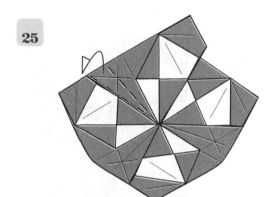

Repeat steps 23–24
three times.

26

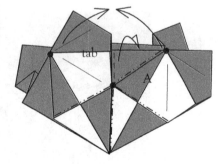

The model closes with a four-way twist
lock. One of four sides is shown. Puff
out at the lower dot, the upper dots will
meet and A will cover the tab.

27

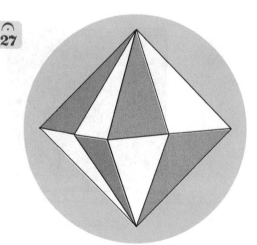

Kaleidoscopic Octahedron

Octahedron with Triangles

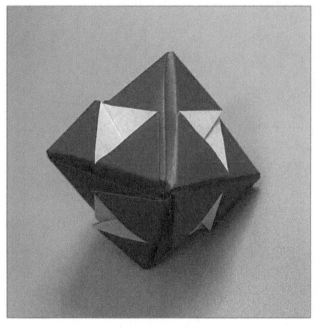

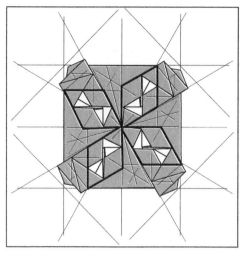

The octahedron has a white triangle in the middle of each face. A pinwheel (step 9) gives the paper for the color changes. This model uses square symmetry and closes with a four-way twist lock.

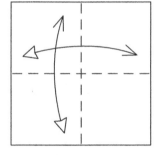

1

Fold and unfold.

2

Fold to the center and unfold.

3

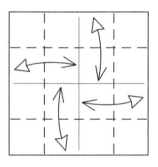

4

Bring the corners to the lines.

5

Fold to the center.

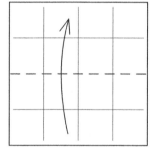

6

Unfold.

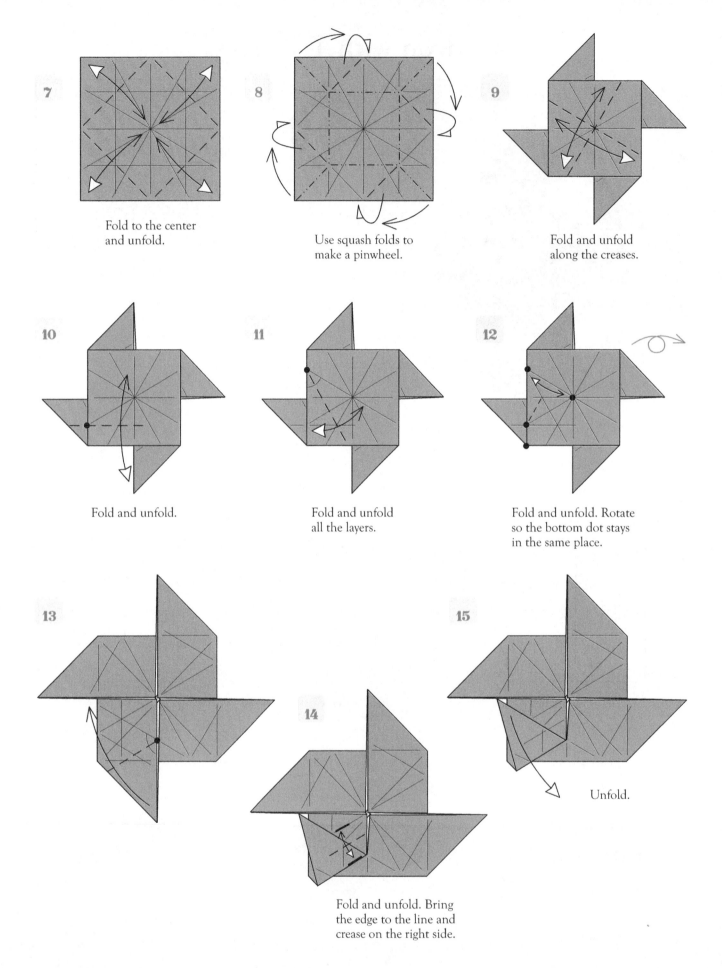

7 Fold to the center and unfold.

8 Use squash folds to make a pinwheel.

9 Fold and unfold along the creases.

10 Fold and unfold.

11 Fold and unfold all the layers.

12 Fold and unfold. Rotate so the bottom dot stays in the same place.

13

14 Fold and unfold. Bring the edge to the line and crease on the right side.

15 Unfold.

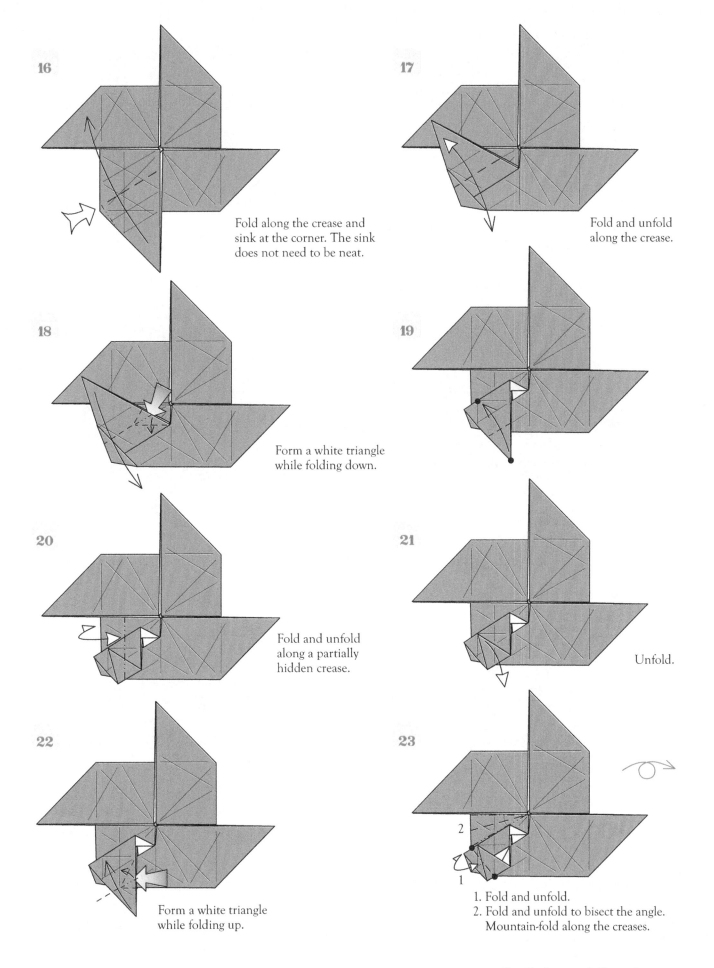

16

Fold along the crease and sink at the corner. The sink does not need to be neat.

17

Fold and unfold along the crease.

18

Form a white triangle while folding down.

19

20

Fold and unfold along a partially hidden crease.

21

Unfold.

22

Form a white triangle while folding up.

23

2

1

1. Fold and unfold.
2. Fold and unfold to bisect the angle.
   Mountain-fold along the creases.

24

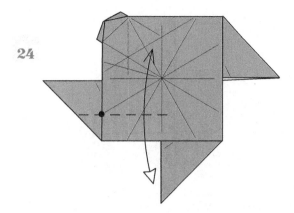

Repeat steps 10–23
three times.

25

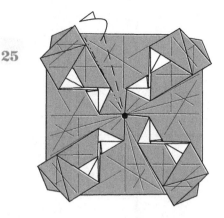

Puff out at the dot.

26

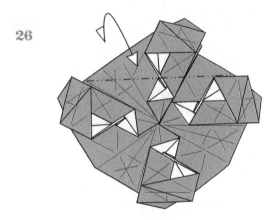

Fold and unfold along
the creases. Rotate 90°.

27

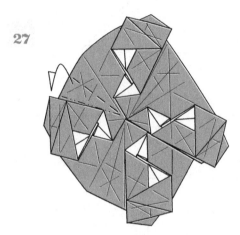

Repeat steps 25–26
three times.

28

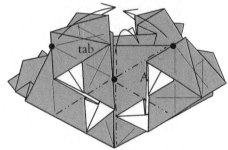

The model closes with a four-way twist
lock. One of four sides is shown. Puff out
at the lower dot, the upper dots will meet
and A will cover the tab.

To do the twist lock, this sequence is done
four times. Since that is difficult, first do
this three times, so three corners meet at
the top. Unfold those and do this again
to another group of three. Then tuck in
the fourth side to lock the model.

29

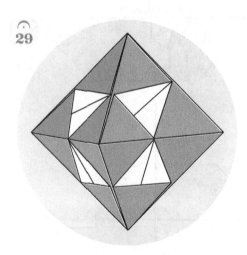

Octahedron
with Triangles

Fourth Movement

Allegro: Sounds of Dangerous Animals

𝄢 We will need some good luck to survive this last movement, so bring some diamonds and a few butterflies from the previous movements. Danger is lurking all around. A Lion and Lioness are hidden but waiting to pounce. A Crocodile, Rhino, Hippo and Hyena are searching for their next meal. Only the brave will survive so fold these carefully. Once these wild animals are fed, they will entertain you with their roars, splashes and laughter.

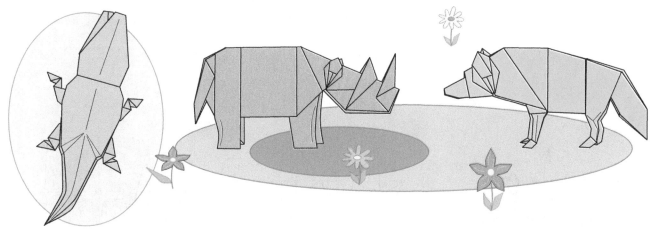

Lion

Lions are a symbol of strength and courage. These apex predators live in grasslands or savannah. Lions sleep 21 hours a day, sometimes resting in trees on low branches. Their roar can be heard for five miles. The mane gets darker as they age. Their lifespan is 10 to 15 years in the wild but longer in captivity.

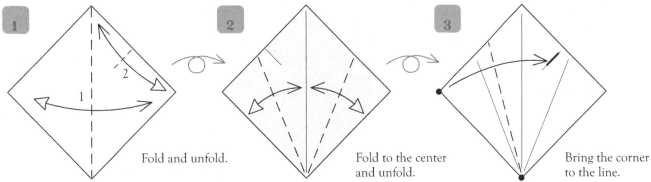

1 Fold and unfold.

2 Fold to the center and unfold.

3 Bring the corner to the line.

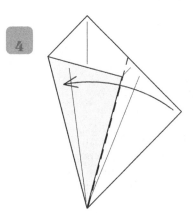

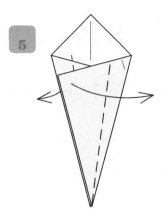

Fold along the creases.

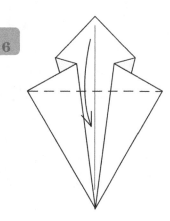

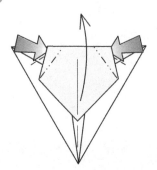

Make squash folds while folding up. Mountain-fold on hidden layers.

Note the equilateral triangle embedded in this shape.

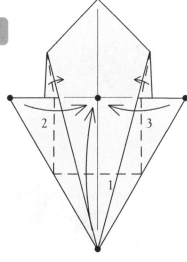

The dots will meet.

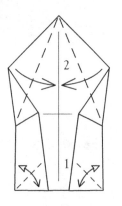

1. Fold and unfold.
2. Fold to the center.

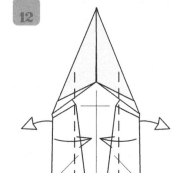

Fold to the center and swing out from behind.

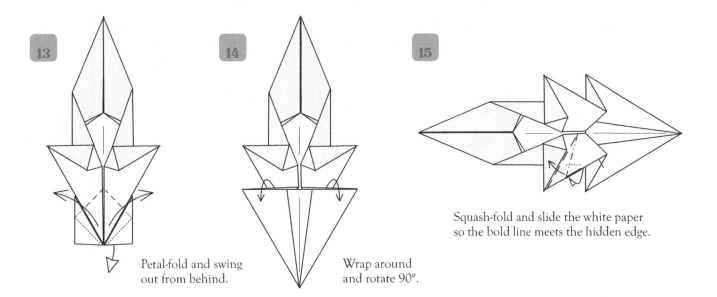

Petal-fold and swing
out from behind.

Wrap around
and rotate 90°.

Squash-fold and slide the white paper
so the bold line meets the hidden edge.

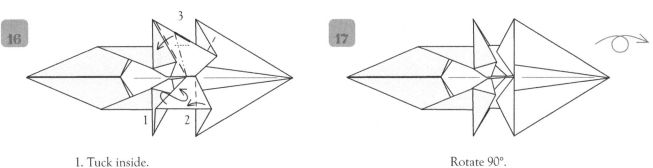

1. Tuck inside.
2. Valley-fold.
3. Repeat steps 15–16 on the top.

Rotate 90°.

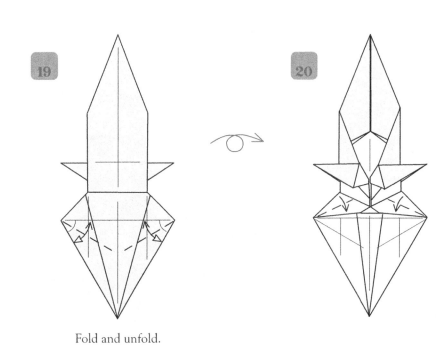

Slide the tail down a
little bit so the edges
on the legs meet.

Fold and unfold.

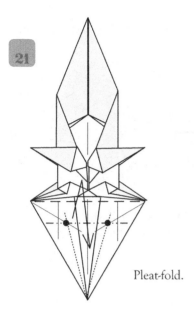

21

Pleat-fold.

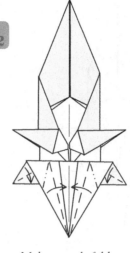

22

Make squash folds.

23

Fold in half and rotate 90°.

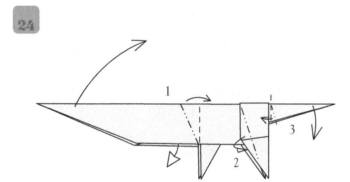

24

1. Crimp-fold and spread on the left, repeat behind.
2. Fold inside, repeat behind.
3. Crimp-fold.

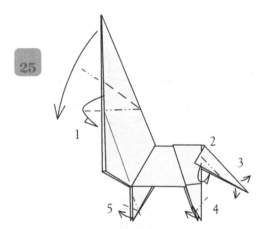

25

1. Crimp-fold.
2. Reverse-fold, repeat behind.
3. Spread the tip of the tail.
4. Reverse-fold, repeat behind.
5. Crimp-fold, repeat behind.

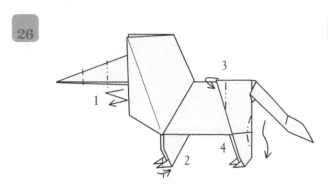

26

1. Crimp-fold.
2. Reverse-fold, repeat behind.
3. Reverse-fold.
4. Shape the legs, repeat behind.

27

Lion

Lioness

The female (lioness) is smaller than the lion and is more agile. The lionesses do most of the hunting, using teamwork to capture prey. As their night vision is far more sensitive than humans, they like to hunt at night. Hunting at night makes it easier to sneak up to its prey which includes zebra, wildebeest and antelope. They can run at speeds of up to 50 miles an hour. Lions and lionesses live in groups of prides. With one or two lions in the pride, most are females. The females take care of the young while the males watch over the pride, protecting it from predators and rival males.

Begin with step 23 of the Lion (page 107).

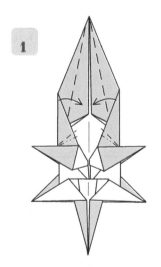

1

Fold to the center.

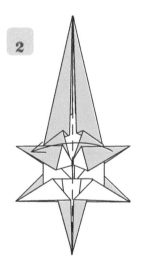

2

Fold in half and rotate 90°.

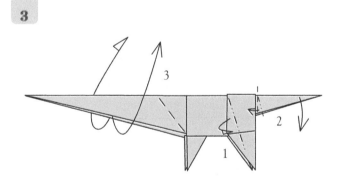

3

1. Fold inside, repeat behind.
2. Crimp-fold.
3. Outside-reverse-fold.

4

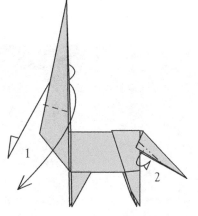

1. Outside-reverse-fold.
2. Reverse-fold, repeat behind.

5

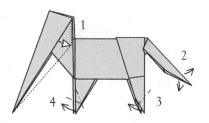

1. Pull out, repeat behind.
2. Spread the tip of the tail.
3. Reverse-fold, repeat behind.
4. Crimp-fold, repeat behind.

6

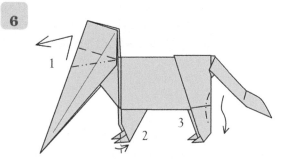

1. Crimp-fold.
2. Reverse-fold, repeat behind.
3. Shape the legs, repeat behind.

7

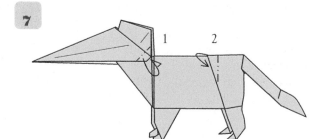

1. Fold behind, repeat behind.
2. Reverse-fold.

8

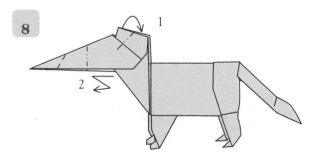

1. Reverse-fold.
2. Crimp-fold.

9

Lioness

Crocodile

Still the same as they were for over 200 million years, crocodiles survived the dinosaurs and continue to thrive. A crocodile can grow to 20 feet and live over 70 years. The mother protects its young for several months. With a large jaw, they have one of the strongest bites of all animals. They can regenerate and replace thousands of teeth during their lifetime. They feed on fish, mammals, birds, and reptiles. They have senses that can detect small changes in the water movements made by prey or threats.

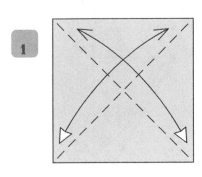

Fold and unfold.

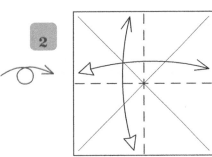

Fold and unfold.

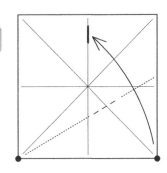

Bring the lower right dot to the bold line. Crease on the diagonal.

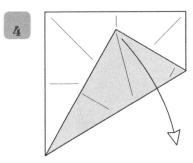

Unfold and rotate 180°.

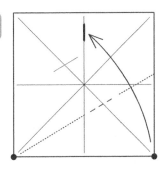

Repeat steps 3–4. Rotate 45°.

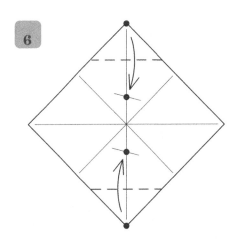

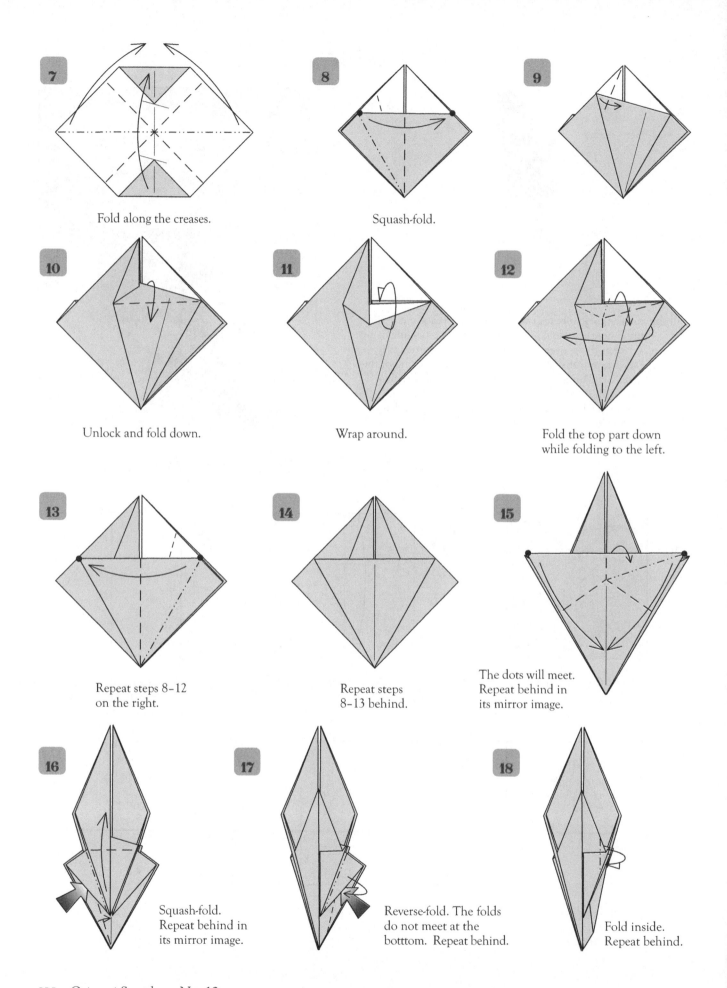

7 Fold along the creases.

8 Squash-fold.

9

10 Unlock and fold down.

11 Wrap around.

12 Fold the top part down while folding to the left.

13 Repeat steps 8–12 on the right.

14 Repeat steps 8–13 behind.

15 The dots will meet. Repeat behind in its mirror image.

16 Squash-fold. Repeat behind in its mirror image.

17 Reverse-fold. The folds do not meet at the botttom. Repeat behind.

18 Fold inside. Repeat behind.

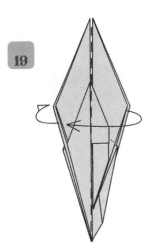

19

Fold one flap to the
left and repeat behind.

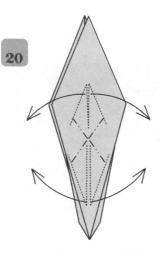

20

Make four reverse folds.

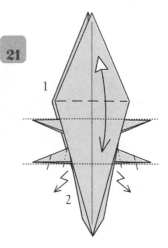

21

Note the legs lie on horizontal lines.
1. Fold and unfold the top flap.
2. Make pleat folds.

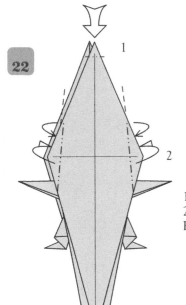

22

1. Sink.
2. Fold inside.
Repeat behind.

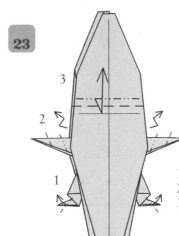

23

1. Spread the feet.
2. Make pleat folds.
3. Pleat-fold all the layers together.

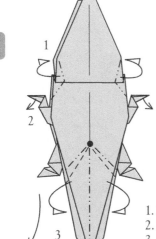

24

1. Fold behind.
2. Spread the feet.
3. Puff out at the dot
   and shape the tail.

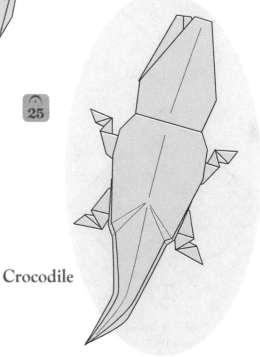

25

Crocodile

Rhinoceros

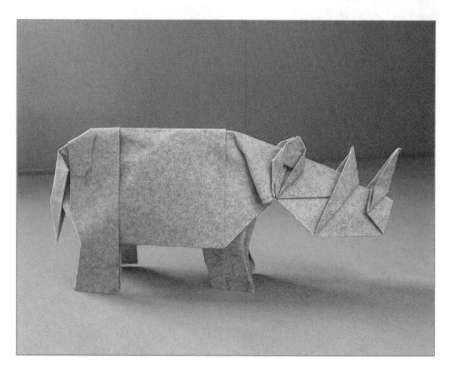

From Ancient Greek, rhinoceros means "nose" (rhino) "horn" (ceros). As the second largest land mammal, they can run at 30 to 40 miles per hour. The White Rhino and Black Rhino have two horns, as depicted by this origami design, yet they are neither white nor black. Rhinos feed on grass, plants, and bushes. Their thick skin protects them like armor. They like to wallow in the mud to keep cool and will wade in shallow water but are not good swimmers. They communicate with grunts, snorts, and trumpet calls.

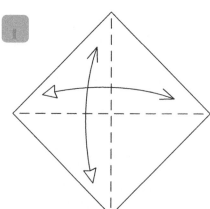

Fold and unfold.

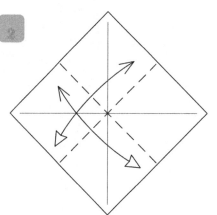

Fold and unfold.

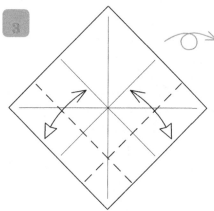

Fold and unfold.

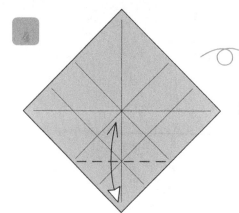

Fold and unfold.
Rotate 180°.

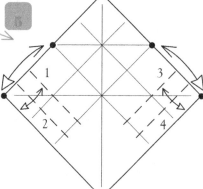

Fold and unfold.
Rotate 180°.

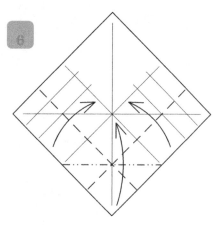

Fold along the creases.

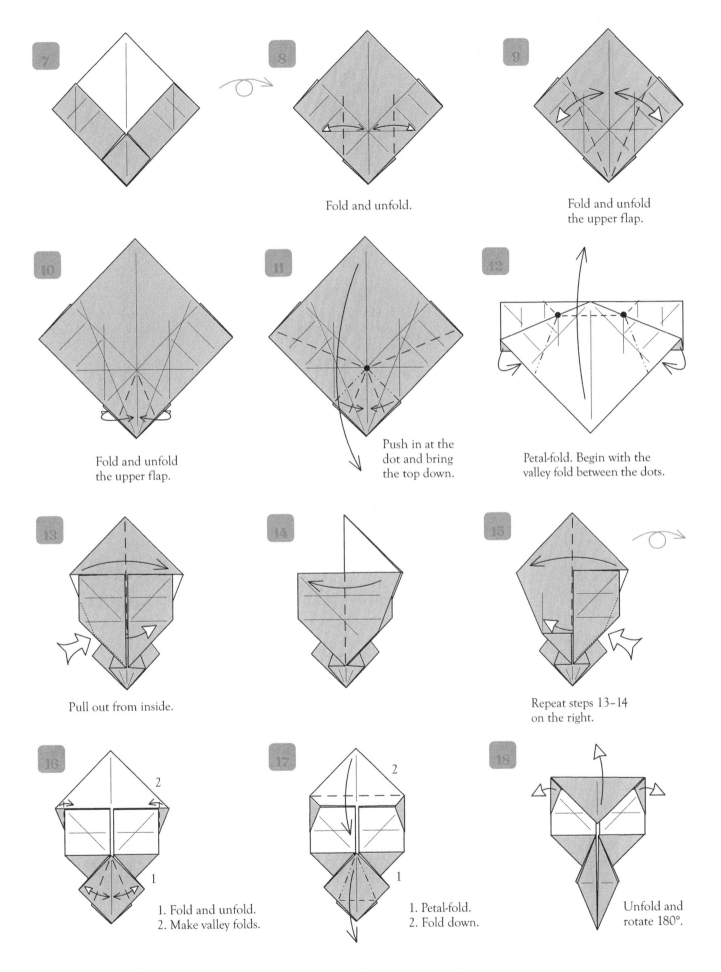

7

8

Fold and unfold.

9

Fold and unfold
the upper flap.

10

Fold and unfold
the upper flap.

11

Push in at the
dot and bring
the top down.

12

Petal-fold. Begin with the
valley fold between the dots.

13

Pull out from inside.

14

15

Repeat steps 13–14
on the right.

16

1. Fold and unfold.
2. Make valley folds.

17

1. Petal-fold.
2. Fold down.

18

Unfold and
rotate 180°.

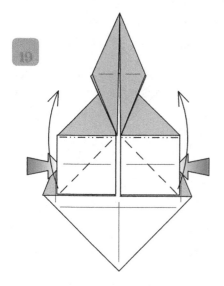

Make reverse folds.

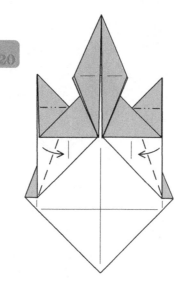

Mountain-fold
along the creases.

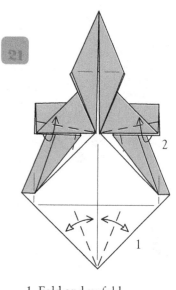

1. Fold and unfold.
2. Make small squash folds.

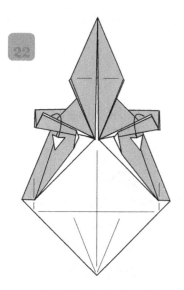

Unfold the top layer.

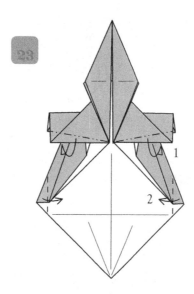

1. Tuck inside.
2. Fold along the creases.

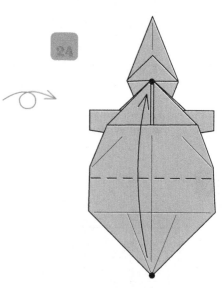

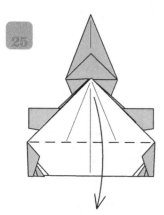

Fold along the crease.

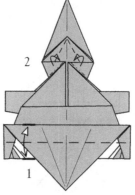
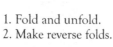

1. Fold and unfold.
2. Make reverse folds.

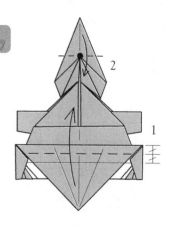

1. Fold up.
2. Fold down.

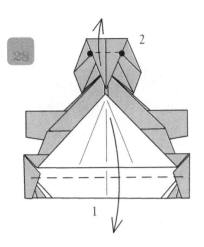

28

1. Fold along the crease.
2. Fold up.

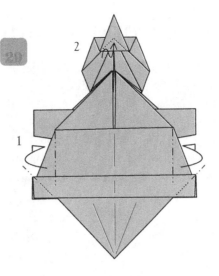

29

1. Make squash folds.
2. Bring the flap to the front.

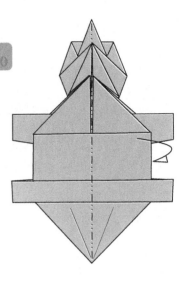

30

Fold in half and rotate 90°.

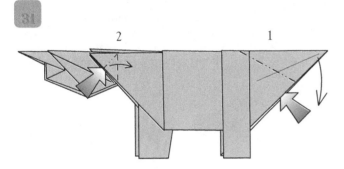

31

1. Reverse-fold.
2. Squash-fold at the second pocket, repeat behind.

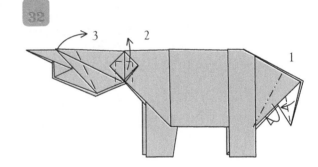

32

1. Reverse-fold, repeat behind.
2. Petal-fold, repeat behind.
3. Outside-reverse-fold.

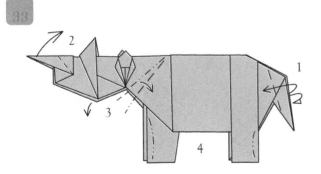

33

1. Outside-reverse-fold.
2. Outside-reverse-fold.
3. Crimp-fold.
4. Shape the legs, repeat behind.

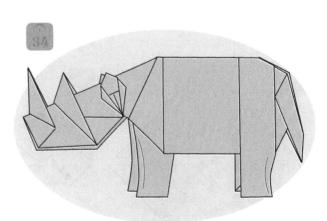

34

Rhinoceros

Hippopotamus

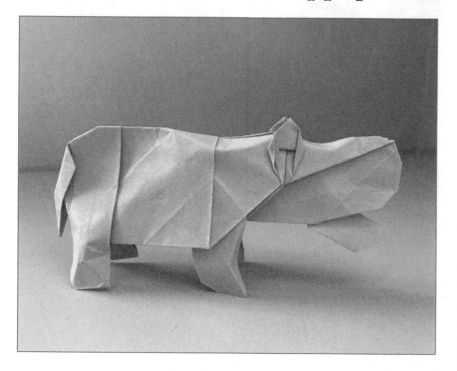

Named from Greek words, hippo (horse) potamus (river) together means "river horse". At 7,000 pounds, they are the third largest land mammal after the elephant and rhino. Their closest relatives are whales and porpoises. They spend most of the day in shallow waters to keep cool. As a herbivore, they feed on grass and other plants, grazing for hours during the cooler night. A group of hippos is a herd or bloat. Hippos are one of the most dangerous of the large animals in Africa and have huge jaws with large canine teeth. They can crush a crocodile or lion with ease, yet their teeth are mainly used for combat rather than feeding. These loud vocal creatures make all sorts of honks, growls, and squeaks.

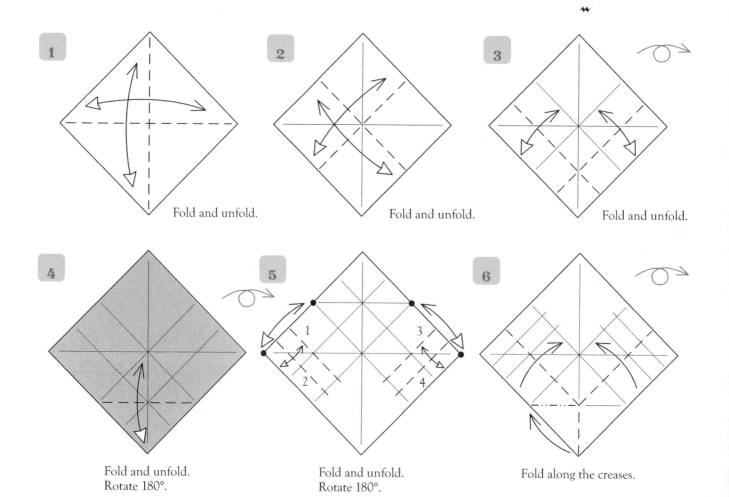

1 Fold and unfold.

2 Fold and unfold.

3 Fold and unfold.

4 Fold and unfold. Rotate 180°.

5 Fold and unfold. Rotate 180°.

6 Fold along the creases.

7

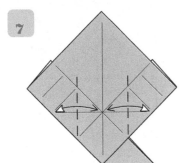

Fold and unfold.

8

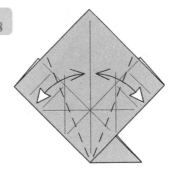

Fold and unfold
the upper flap.

9

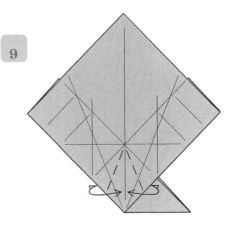

Fold and unfold
the upper flap.

10

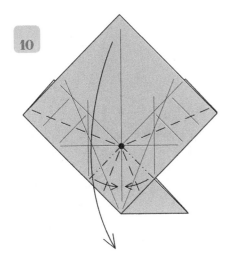

Push in at the dot and
bring the top down.

11

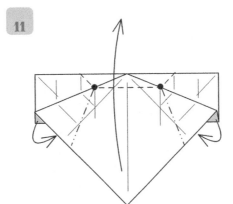

Petal-fold. Begin with the
valley fold between the dots.

12

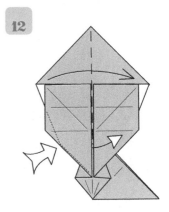

Pull out from inside.

13

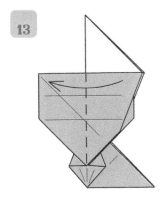

14

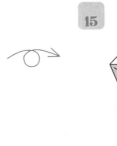

Repeat steps 12–13
on the right.

15

2

1

1. Fold on the
   left and right.
2. Fold down.

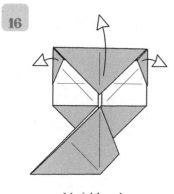

16

Unfold and
rotate 180°.

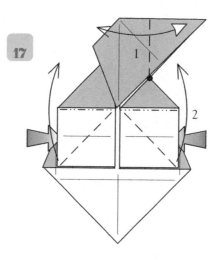

17

1. Fold and unfold.
2. Make reverse folds.

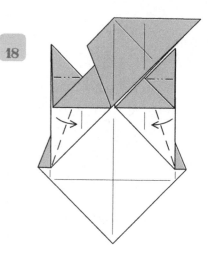

18

Mountain-fold
along the creases.

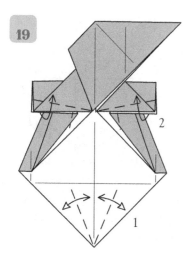

19

1. Fold and unfold.
2. Make small squash folds.

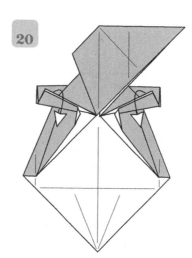

20

Unfold the top layer.

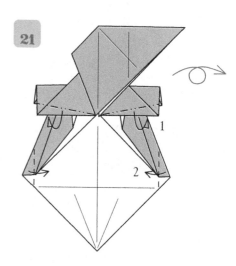

21

1. Tuck inside.
2. Fold along the creases.

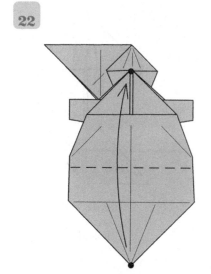

22

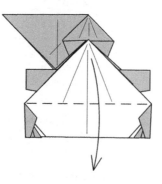

23

Fold along the crease.

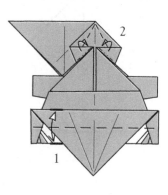

24

1. Fold and unfold.
2. Make reverse folds.

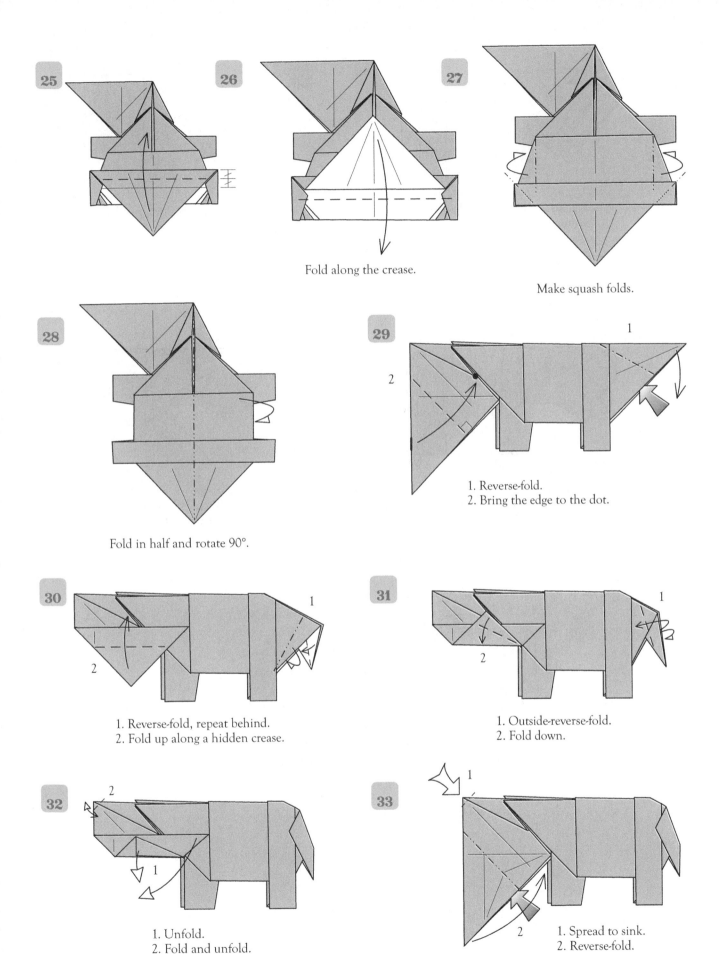

Fold along the crease.

Make squash folds.

Fold in half and rotate 90°.

1. Reverse-fold.
2. Bring the edge to the dot.

1. Reverse-fold, repeat behind.
2. Fold up along a hidden crease.

1. Outside-reverse-fold.
2. Fold down.

1. Unfold.
2. Fold and unfold.

1. Spread to sink.
2. Reverse-fold.

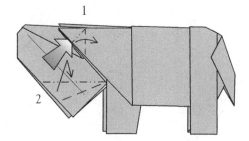

1. Squash-fold at the second pocket.
2. Crimp-fold.
Repeat behind.

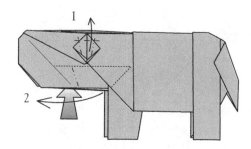

1. Petal-fold, repeat behind.
2. Reverse-fold.

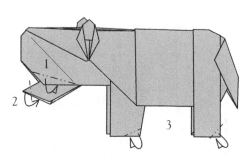

1. Fold inside, repeat behind.
2. Reverse-fold.
3. Fold behind, repeat behind.

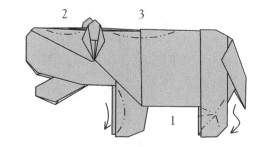

1. Shape the legs, repeat behind.
2. Shape the head.
3. Shape the back.

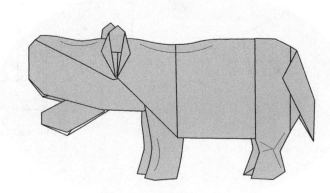

Hippopotamus

Hyena

Hyenas are intelligent and curious social animals that live in large clans. Working in packs, they hunt prey by running up to 37 miles per hour, as they exhaust their prey. They capture large animals such as wildebeest, antelope, and zebra along with smaller animals like hares and birds. They are also scavengers and eat everything including bone and horn. They often look up in the sky for clues from vultures. Their enemies include lions and crocodiles. Living from 12 to 20 years, they make interesting laughing sounds.

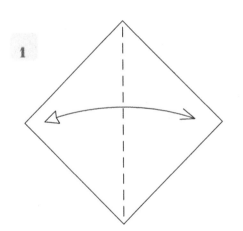

1

Fold and unfold.

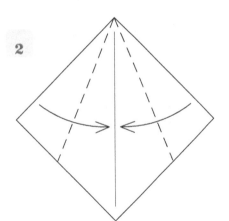

2

Fold to the center.

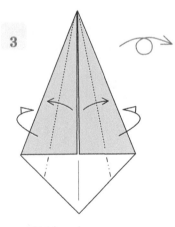

3

Fold to the center and swing out.

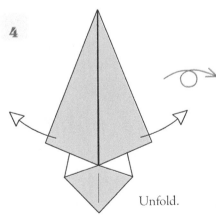

4

Unfold.

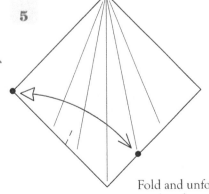

5

Fold and unfold on the edge.

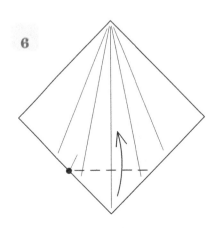

6

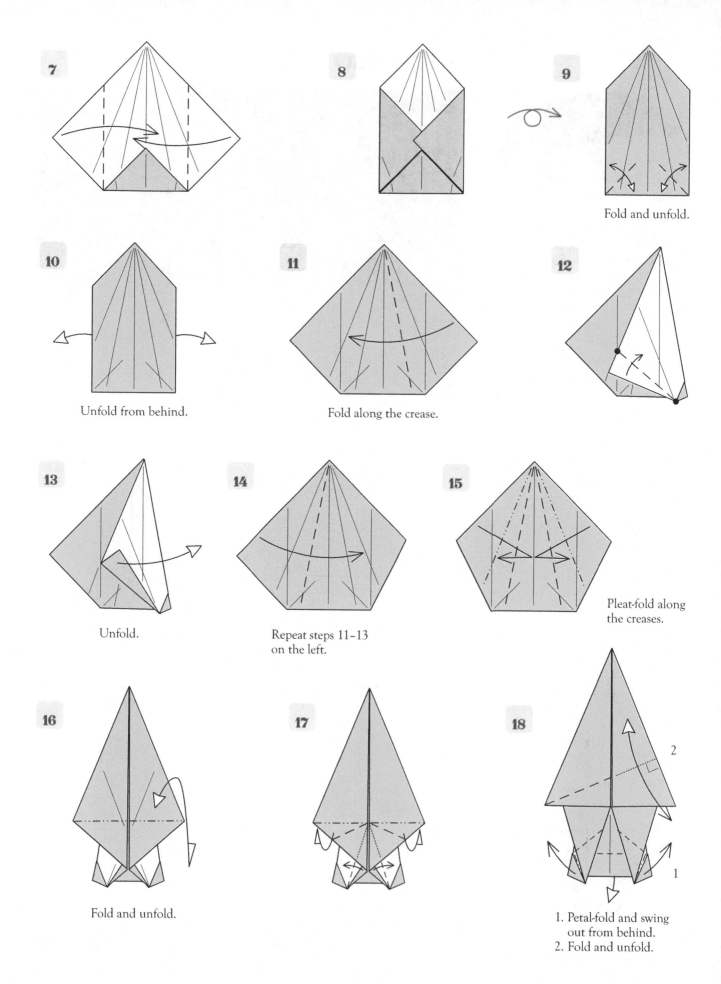

7

8

9

Fold and unfold.

10

Unfold from behind.

11

Fold along the crease.

12

13

Unfold.

14

Repeat steps 11–13 on the left.

15

Pleat-fold along the creases.

16

Fold and unfold.

17

18

2

1

1. Petal-fold and swing out from behind.
2. Fold and unfold.

19

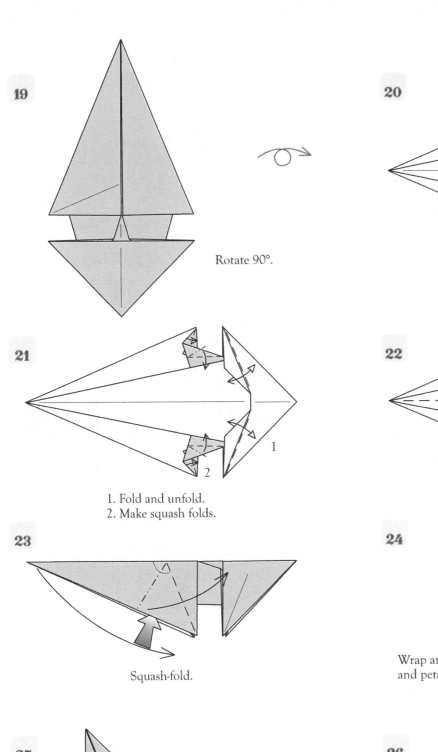

Rotate 90°.

20

21

1. Fold and unfold.
2. Make squash folds.

22

Fold in half.

23

Squash-fold.

24

Wrap around
and petal-fold.

25

1. Fold and unfold.
2. Reverse-fold.

26

1. Fold in half to form the neck.
2. Wrap around the tail, repeat behind.

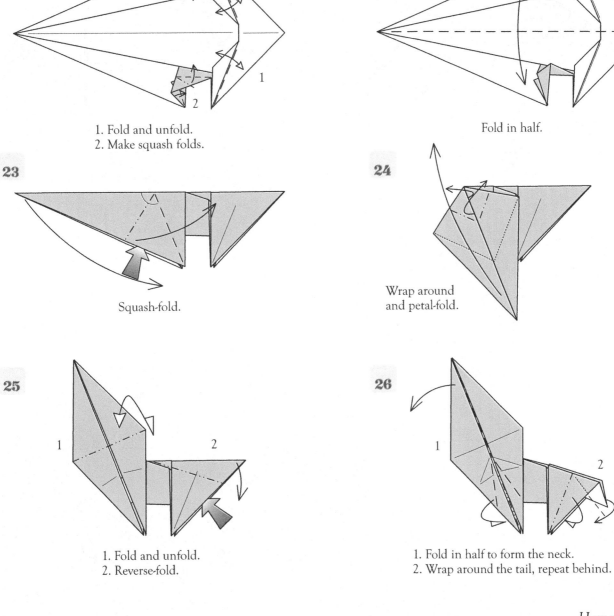

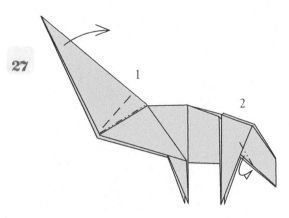

27

1. Valley-fold along the crease for this crimp fold.
2. Make a small hidden squash fold, repeat behind.

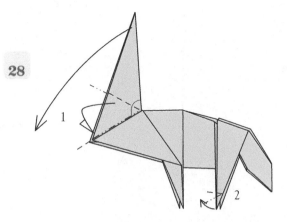

28

1. Crimp-fold.
2. Squash-fold, repeat behind.

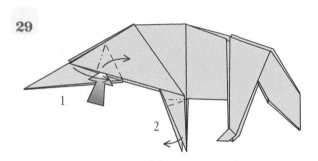

29

1. Squash-fold.
2. Crimp-fold.
Repeat behind.

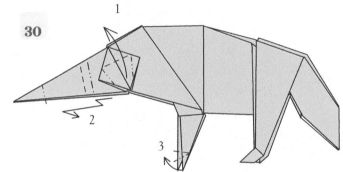

30

1. Petal-fold, repeat behind.
2. Crimp and reverse-fold.
3. Squash-fold, repeat behind.

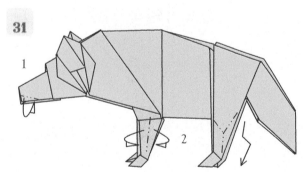

31

1. Fold inside.
2. Shape the legs.
Repeat behind.

32

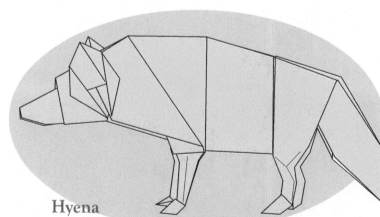

Hyena

Made in the USA
Las Vegas, NV
23 June 2024